Counterespionage for American Business

Peter Pitorri, M.A., CPP

Butterworth-Heinemann
Boston   Oxford   Johannesburg   Melbourne   New Delhi   Singapore

Butterworth–Heinemann supports the efforts of American Forests and the Global ReLeaf program in its campaign for the betterment of trees, forests, and our environment.

Library of Congress Cataloging-in-Publication Data

Pitorri, Peter, 1938–
    Counterespionage for American business / Peter Pitorri.
        p.   cm.
    Includes index.
    ISBN 0-7506-7044-4 (pbk. : alk. paper)
    1. Business intelligence—United States.   2. Industries—Security
measures—United States.   I. Title.
    HD38.7.P58   1998
    658.4'7—dc21   98-9708
                                                                                        CIP

British Library Cataloguing-in-Publication Data
A catalogue record for this book is available from the British Library.

The publisher offers special discounts on bulk orders of this book.
For information, please contact:
Manager of Special Sales
Butterworth–Heinemann
225 Wildwood Avenue
Woburn, MA 01801-2041
Tel: 781-904-2500
Fax: 781-904-2620

For information on all Butterworth–Heinemann books available,
contact our World Wide Web home page at: http://www.bh.com

10 9 8 7 6 5 4 3 2 1

Printed in the United States of America

Text books usually do not bear dedications, but I have promises to keep and miles to go before I sleep.

To my wife, Rosanne, whose patience, love, and caring have supported me through three careers. Love's Labours Won.

To my friend, Lloyd Reese (very likely the only one left), whose erudite criticism and old-fashioned friendship serve as my lighthouse in the fog of wisdom. The tide in the affairs of men, taken at the flood, leads to fortune.

To my former Director for Intelligence and Security, Colonel Richard N. Armstrong, United States Army (Retired), whose encouragement made me be all the writer I could be, so that I could share forty years of experience and training. Agent handling takes on a whole new meaning.

Contents

About the Author

Peter Pitorri is a Certified Protection Professional (CPP). During a twenty-nine-year career in Federal service, he served as an intelligence analyst, intelligence agent, operations security manager, counterintelligence specialist, antiterrorism instructor, and security investigator (internal affairs). He served during the Cold War in Europe and the hot war in Vietnam. He is a member of the American Society for Industrial Security (ASIS). He is a Diplomate in the Department of Defense Security Specialist Program, and a graduate of nine other intelligence, counterintelligence, and security programs. Pitorri has a Master of Arts degree in security management.

A columnist and freelance writer, Pitorri has published widely on information and personnel security management. He has presented lectures, seminars, and workshops before ASIS, the National Computer Security Association, the National Operations Security Society, the University of Delaware, Northern Virginia Community College, and various corporate clients.

In his spare time, he operates a security management firm and tends to his tropical fish.

Preface

While there is a plethora of manuals and loss-prevention (LP) books written for security practitioners, I have found none written for the very people they serve: corporate America and the legal profession. That is why I wrote this minimanual of tips about and techniques of counterespionage (or CE—also called counterintelligence or CI by the military services). It is for the management population of American business, industry, and institutions who need to protect their assets but don't know how. It is for the law firms—primarily the single-lawyer and small firms—that practice corporate law, or would like to.

I have written this book for you, because many of you do not know how to manage loss prevention and, thus, cannot protect your assets; because all of you are exposed to the legal consequences of negligent hiring and inadequate security; and because foreign governments are stealing American business secrets.

This book will identify the foreign espionage threat to American business. It will reveal espionage collection methods (called tradecraft). It will show you how to identify and correct your vulnerabilities to espionage and other types of loss.

You will learn that cost-effective counterespionage programs begin with the weakest link in security: people. You cannot just lock up your trade secrets and expect them to be safe, unless you have employees who are not vulnerable to blackmail, political pressure, financial and sexual inducements, and more. Industrial espionage succeeds only through the subversion of people.

This book will teach you CI methods for screening your employment applicants. You will learn how to use standard screening methods to defend against not only industrial espionage but also violent persons.

Finally, you can use this book to design your security education program. Your employees may not care about the details of counterespionage, but they do care about their jobs. You need to teach them that if they treat trade secrets carelessly, they risk losing of their jobs. But you must also teach them how to protect those trade secrets. This book will help you do all of that.

Let me make it easy for you to decide if you want to buy this book. Do you want to know how to protect your firm's proprietary information from being compromised, or being stolen by a foreign power? Do you want to prevent an employee or former employee from killing someone on your property? Do you want to learn how spies recruit spies within your company? Do you want to find out which countries are stealing your information? If you answered "Yes" to any of these questions, then buy this book now.

Peter Pitorri, M.A., CPP
United States Army Intelligence (Ret.)

Introduction

After years of intensive research, I have learned that you, the executives and managers of American business, often don't think about security. Your principal concern is the bottom line. That's okay. That's America. But you do have a problem. Although you all know how to make money, few of you know how to protect it from loss. Your firms frequently lose money through the loss of critical information, and through lawsuits for liability. These would be serious problems at any time, but in today's market, these problems will become catastrophic if left unchecked.

American business is competing in a world market where competitors win million-dollar contracts by bid margins of a few hundred dollars. But there's no great skill involved in these bidding wars, for companies often buy or even steal other companies' bid strategies. In fact, they often buy these strategies from employees.

Moreover, you hire imperfect strangers without knowing anything about them—without verifying their skills, education, experience, or criminal records. Many of you have lost lawsuits for negligent hiring because of the damage to others caused by a few unscreened employees. For example, clean-cut young American males compromise the confidentiality, integrity, and availability of your critical business information. They do it for many reasons. *This manual will show you who they are, why they do it, and how they do it.* This manual will show you how to prevent the loss of your critical business information, and how to avoid liability for negligent hiring.

Foreign governments, on behalf of their industries, also conduct aggressive espionage against American firms. Are you concerned that your high technology and biotechnology—the fruits of American research—may become the assets of foreign powers? Of course you are. *This manual will show you who those foreign powers are, what information they're after, and how they're stealing it.*

American business is about productivity. Loss prevention is about identifying those factors that reduce productivity in order to eliminate or control them. That's another thing this manual is about—*control:* how to exercise it, and how not to. Hiring employees without verifying their backgrounds constitutes very little control. I think that you will appreciate my formula for increasing productivity via increased control over loss in Chapter 7.

To increase the productivity of your company, you will learn how to increase the probability that each individual admitted onto your premises is trustworthy. If people are trustworthy, they probably will not lie, steal, kill, or compromise your trade secrets. You will learn how to verify someone's claimed skills in order to avoid having to terminate a recent hire who cannot fulfill the promises of his résumé.

You will learn as well the role played by statistical probability in loss-prevention management. We cannot protect against the possibility of loss. For example, what's the possibility that someone is breaking into your home at this moment? What's the possibility that you or a loved one will be car-jacked? These possibilities are scary to contemplate, because there is no way to forecast the *possibility* of a threat and, thereby, issue a warning. But probability can be calculated; it's a statistical function. *The prevention of loss is based on the probability of occurrence of loss-inducing events.*

When you practice loss-prevention or LP management, you protect your two most important assets, people and information. You protect your market share and provide a return on your investment by focusing on the five steps of risk assessment: identify and evaluate your assets; analyze your threats; analyze your vulnerabilities; analyze the impact or benefit-cost; and recommend improvement options. The section on risk assessment in Chapter 2, explains in detail what these steps are and how to use them. In this discussion you will discover a vital technique for protecting your assets. You will note immediately that the technique has three key features:

1. It is methodical.
2. It is objective.
3. It gets measurable results.

ABOVE ALL, *CARE*

While you're reading, keep two facts in mind. First of all, *Change is tough*. As soon as you acquire or upgrade a security program, you make life tough for your people. So think about managing change. Think about it while you're looking for a security consultant or guard company or any other security resource. Will the resources help your firm manage change? You can't afford to make life tough for the people who are making money for you—your employees.

Secondly, *Education is an investment*. It's the spoonful of sugar that makes the change go down. An education program is the foundation of all productive change. Education makes a loss prevention program work. Education develops the resources you already have and provides an identifiable long-term return on your investment.

Counterespionage—
Your Mini-Manual

The most cost-effective approach to R & D is to steal trade secrets.
...Yvonne M. Kisiel, *Security Management* (May 1990)

Industrial espionage (IE) is costing U.S. business $100 billion/year in lost sales (White House Office of Science & Technology, October 28, 1997).

Your firm faces three industrial espionage threats:

1. There are over 3,000 foreign espionage agents in the United States.
2. Some nations that have been historically friendly to the United States steal your critical technology.
3. Some of your competitors steal from you.

The Soviet Union collapsed in 1990. The Commonwealth of Independent States consists of eleven nations in competition with each other and the West. The foreign operations of the Russian KGB and GRU have not been reduced. Although its name has changed (see Appendix A), the KGB (as Americans know it) is still the state security agency charged with, among other things, collecting foreign intelligence in science and technology. The GRU is the Russian military intelligence agency (see Appendix A for details). These agencies may have been streamlined and had some of their names changed, but some of their spying efforts have been increased by as much as 100%! They steal biotechnology and high technology secrets to help their economy survive. And the Eastern nations are not the only foreign intelligence threat to U.S. business. (For more details regarding foreign countries and their espionage efforts, see Appendix A.)

In 1990, a source cited as a senior FBI official commented that "France spied on IBM and Texas Instruments . . . [It was] very aggressive in its IE efforts against other U.S. electronics companies" (*New York Times*, November 18, 1990). As you will see, industrial espionage conducted by the French government against American business has intensified during the six years since that remark was published.

Israel coldly accepted the fruits of Jonathan Pollard's traitorous activities. As we shall see, he was a naval counterterrorism analyst who sold that country more than 1,000 classified documents containing priceless American high technology secrets. This was odd behavior for a country that was covertly given nuclear technology and assisted in its development by the United States.

According to Peter Schweitzer, author of *Friendly Spies: How America's Allies are Using Economic Espionage to Steal Our Secrets* (1993), agents of Mitsubishi and Hitachi reportedly paid $650,000 for information on the IBM 3081. U.S. counterintelligence experts tell us that Japan has been stealing American industrial secrets for over thirty years.

Historically, Japan has had the most aggressive industrial espionage base in the world. It has been supported by nearly limitless government funds. The interesting point is that the government of Japan has had no foreign intelligence operations since the end of World War II. All of its intelligence gathering has been conducted by Japanese industry. Until recently, that is, when the Japanese government created a triservice Intelligence Headquarters. It is to be headed by a three-star general and staffed by 1,200 military and civilian workers. Its budget for 1996 was reported to be $56.6 million (*Defense News*, February 5–11, 1996).

THE THREAT FROM WITHIN

Industrial espionage has resulted in losses of billions of dollars of information and the compromise of some of America's most precious secrets.

You don't read about the dollar losses incurred by private industry. If you were the CEO of a company that had just given up $1.75 million in research secrets, or three and a half years' worth of marketing research to a foreign government, would you call a press conference? Of course not. Neither did the two Fortune 500 firms that suffered these incidents in 1995.

But we do read about the losses incurred by some government contractors and the American government via the traitorous activities of a few employees. It has happened to Northrop, Hughes Aircraft, IBM, TRW, Texas Instruments, Dow Corning, the NSA (National Security Agency), the CIA, the Naval Investigative Service, and others. Here are just a few examples of successful espionage activities.

Thomas Cavanagh was an engineering specialist at Northrop. He had serious financial and domestic problems, and frequently lied to his employer and co-workers. He contacted Soviet representatives in Los Angeles, offering to sell high technology secrets concerning the Stealth bomber. He was arrested by the FBI in December of 1984 and is serving two concurrent life terms.

William Bell was a project manager of the Radar Systems Group for Hughes Aircraft in El Segundo, California. Bell lost his son in an accident, lost his wife in a painful divorce, and was about to declare bankruptcy. He sought a way out of financial distress by selling high technology secrets concerning sophisticated radar and other systems to the Polish Intelligence Service. Bell was arrested by the FBI in June of 1981 and served eight years.

In 1977, Christopher Boyce and Andrew Daulton Lee, employees of TRW Inc. in California, sold top secret communications codes to the Soviet KGB for $70,000. This traitorous activity compromised critical American surveillance satellite systems. (For more information about Boyce and Lee, see Appendix A.)

Ronald Pelton, a communications specialist with the National Security Agency for fourteen years, was identified as a spy for the Soviet Union (and a traitor to the U.S.) by the Soviet defector Vitaly Yurchenko in 1985. Pelton sold classified intelligence collection information to the KGB for some $35,000. He was indicted on six counts related to espionage, and was convicted on one count of conspiracy and two counts of espionage. He is serving three concurrent life sentences.

Aldrich Hazen Ames, a CIA intelligence officer, sold information to the Soviet KGB and its successor, the Ministry of Security for the Russian Federation; this classified information cost the lives of nearly twenty CIA agents. He received close to $2.5 million from his Soviet and Russian handlers during a period of nine years. Ames was arrested by the FBI in February, 1994, and sentenced to life imprisonment without parole.

Jonathan Pollard, as mentioned earlier, was a counterterrorism analyst for the Naval Investigative Service. He contacted an Israeli military officer, and eventually provided secret and top secret high technology to Israel. After being arrested by the FBI in November 1985, he admitted to planning similar deals with the Peoples Republic of China. Pollard is serving a life term. Israel continues to aggressively collect both industrial and political intelligence from the United States, both overtly and by means of deception.

It is important to note that a spy is a government agent who collects information of strategic political or economic value about a foreign power while operating in the target country on behalf of his or her own government. The people cited above were traitors, not spies.

WHO'S STEALING YOUR SECRETS: IDENTIFYING THE THREAT

In *The Washington Times* (October 7, 1996), under the subhead "Economic spy blitz by Russia expected," staff writer Bill Gertz wrote, "U.S. counterintelligence officials are bracing for increased spying by Russia's intelligence service as a result of a report that the KGB is reorganizing to focus more on collecting U.S. and Western economic secrets." These U.S. officials were, I'm afraid, a few years behind. The Russian intelligence agencies reorganized for this purpose nearly six years ago. Gertz goes on to say, "The new goals of the spy agency . . . include increased efforts . . . to gather economic, scientific, and technical information." In fact, those goals have been in place since 1990; before that time, Soviet spy operations concerned themselves primarily with political and military information.

In *The Dallas Morning News* (October 7, 1996), under the subhead "Foreign spies target corporate secrets," staff writer Jim Landers reported:

> Economic espionage is booming. . . . U.S. firms have suffered losses to spies from China, France, Canada, India, Japan, Germany, South Korea, Israel, and Taiwan. . . . The CIA has identified Russia, France, Iran, China, Israel, and Cuba as governments most engaged in American industrial espionage.

Here, for the first time in print, is a list I have compiled from public sources over the last fifteen years of the countries that are known to be customers of stolen U.S. technology:

Argentina

Brazil

France

India

Iran

Iraq

Israel

Japan

Lebanon

Libya

North Korea

Pakistan

Peoples Republic of China (PRC)

Russia/USSR

South Africa

South Korea

Taiwan

This list is current as of November 1996. Some of the governments of these countries, such as France, Iraq, Israel, and the PRC, consider the United States to be a primary target for industrial and economic collection activities (i.e., espionage). Others, such as Iran, Libya, and Russia, engage third parties to maintain collection platforms on their behalf. The latter approach is frequently a synergistic relationship. For example, a Middle Eastern foreign power recently needed specific information regarding the preservation of food under extreme heat conditions, but it lacked the ability to collect information (i.e., conduct espionage) in the United States, so it turned to another country within its political and environmental cradle. That second country "piggybacked" the collection requirement on its own agents already in place in the United States. It reaped extraordinary benefit from the low additional cost of this collection effort: it now knows how to process fresh foods for frozen storage, how to maintain that storage, and how best to transport these foods to its troops engaged in combat outside its borders.

There was one little quirk to this operation that James Bond would have loved. The country doing the actual spying withheld portions of the collected intelligence from its client. The collector, for example, did not report to its client the techniques for acquiring or processing the refrigerant itself.

France has been conducting aggressive industrial and economic espionage against the United States since 1981. Pierre Marion, the retired head of the French secret service, told an NBC news correspondent in 1991 that in military and political matters "we are allies. In industrial and economic matters, we are not allies; we are competitors" (NBC Nightly News with Tom Brokaw, September 13, 1991). Marion went on to say that in 1981 he had assigned twenty French secret service agents to intercept telephone calls from American businessmen residing in Paris and to "examine their documents." According to U.S. Intelligence sources, the method for examining those documents consisted of surreptitiously entering hotel rooms that were rented to American businessmen in order to photograph business documents that they had left behind while they were sightseeing or at dinner. American businessmen were (and are—until they read this book) trustful of the French government.

In September 1996, Philippe A. Clerc, an official of the French Office of Economic and Financial Intelligence, reinforced the position of the French government to an American audience at Tysons Corner, Virginia. I recorded the following excerpts from his speech:

> It is very stimulating for me to have the opportunity to share experience at a time when the reality of international competition too often makes of partnership a confrontation.
>
> Economic intelligence [is] . . . all the coordinated measures of research, processing, dissemination, and protection of accurate and workable information obtained through legal means and open sources.
>
> Economic intelligence becomes a technique to interpret and understand the realities of the markets and the different mentalities of competitors and partners, their cultures, *their intentions, and their capacity to implement them* [emphasis added].
>
> In early 1995 the Secretariat General de la Defense Nationale, an administration under the Prime Minister's authority, suggested that the government create a committee for competitiveness and economic security . . . This decree of April 1995 was published with a report to the President of the Republic, that clearly mentioned the will of the State to place competitiveness and information management as an important national challenge.
>
> The committee for competitiveness and economic security is chaired by the Prime Minister, who for the present time delegated his authority in regards to this function to Mr. Jean Arthuis, the Economy and Finances minister.

Clerc went on to say that during a twelve-month period, the French government trained approximately 300 agents in the *collection and analysis of foreign information regarding economics, scientific and technological developments, information security, and the use of databases and the Internet*. I think that a reasonable, prudent person would conclude that American business is a target of French industrial espionage. While the revelation provided by Clerc is not alarming on its own merit, when considered with all the other information we have on French collection operations, it is an indicator of French espionage efforts. This information, coming as it does from a well-placed, knowledgeable source, reinforces the conclusions previously drawn by American intelligence analysts concerning the French espionage threat to American business.

INDUSTRIAL ESPIONAGE TARGET— *YOUR FIRM*

Tradecraft: How Spies Spy

Spies operate by exploiting vulnerabilities. They compromise people by identifying and taking advantage of their weaknesses, whether those weaknesses involve sex, money, criminal activities, or other factors. They compromise businesses by studying their operations and the weaknesses inherent in them. Here are the most significant vulnerabilities that I have found in American businesses:

- *Telephone.* The most useful instrument of espionage. It can be rigged to transmit not only your telephone conversations, but all room conversations—*while the handset is in the cradle!*
- *Fax.* Facsimile machines transmit critical information over telephone lines. Some firms actually send proprietary data by fax. Bad idea.
- *Computer + Modem.* The modem transmits your critical information over telephone lines.
- *Trash.* I'll bet that right this minute, your trash contains information another country or firm could use.
- *Employees.* Some employees sell anything for the right price.
- *Salespersons.* They like to talk about their company. Sometimes too much. These last two vulnerabilities, employees and salespersons, constitute HUMINT or human intelligence sources. When locals are recruited, HUMINT collection may be the least expensive and the most cost-effective intelligence collection platform. In Chapter 4, you will learn how foreign spies recruit local agents—perhaps within your firm. You will learn how employee susceptibility to recruitment is directly related to employee screening.

By the Way . . .

In case you haven't divined this information by now, here are three critical facts for you to keep in mind as you proceed through this manual:

1. Friendly foreign governments steal our secrets to give to their industries.
2. Competitors use the same methods to conduct industrial espionage as foreign governments use.
3. You can't tell by looking at someone if he's going to steal your secrets.

If you're a corporate officer, you probably have a fiduciary responsibility to your board of directors, and through them, to your stockholders. Protecting your critical business information is not an affront to anyone's integrity, it's good business—and self-preservation.

IDENTIFYING THE COVERT AVENUES OF APPROACH TO YOUR INFORMATION

These are the most popular ones, in order of use:

1. Telephone and telecopy (fax) intercept
2. Trash analysis
3. Employee sellouts (subversion)
4. Surreptitious listening devices (bugs)
5. Penetrations (clandestine insertion of an agent into a targeted company)

It's important that you understand order of use. A *telephone intercept* is the most cost-effective for the agent because it is the safest, the easiest, and the most fruitful. Telecopies are sent over voice-grade telephone lines, and are as vulnerable as verbal telephonic exchanges. Telephone intercepts are, thus, the most commonly used form of gathering information.

Trash analysis is the least expensive and is relatively safe. I could hire someone for very little money to give me your trash for later analysis. The yield is extraordinarily rich, so it's number 2.

Employees can *sell out* or be blackmailed. That's another reason for you to insist on pre-employment screening and psychological testing.

Bugs—ah, what can I say. The correct terms are special electronic devices, or surreptitious listening devices, or remote intelligence collection devices, or—well, that's why we call 'em "bugs." Forget the movies and consider the facts: Bugging could be the most lucrative of all forms of information collection, next to telephone intercept, because the listener obtains hard intelligence from primary sources in a timely manner. But it always involves breaking and entering. Well, usually. Otherwise, someone on the inside has to be subverted. Again, contrary to what you see in the movies, breaking and entering, as well as subversion, are risky, so they are seldom used. Also, it costs a small fortune to obtain optimum results from electronic surveillance, so I put bugs in fourth place. But listen, bugs—room, car, and phone—are the "best by test," as we say in the CI business, for timely, accurate intelligence.

If a full electronic surveillance operation is mounted against your firm, two conditions prevail: First, since someone is willing to spend megabucks, you obviously have information someone is desperate to get. Second, *they're going to get everything you have.* Guaranteed. Unless, of course, you call in a Technical Surveillance Countermeasures (TSCM) team. More on this in a moment.

Penetrations are a last resort and the least used. A highly skilled, well-trained spy obtains employment in your firm. This person is not a subverted American agent and is never a U.S. citizen; he's an employee of a foreign government or industry. Once inside, he will recommend to his handler or case officer other effective measures from the preceding list. This method of industrial espionage is expensive and time-consuming. Remember what I said earlier about coercion. It is cheaper and safer for a foreign country to "turn" or corrupt a foreign national who is already working for your company than to place a professional spy inside. In this case, a foreign national is a person without United States citizenship who is a resident in this country. So we have three HUMINT sources: the professional foreign spy; the coerced foreign national; and the disaffected American employee.

OVERT COLLECTION

This is one more way to collect information about competitors. It is also called open source reviews or, more accurately, competitor intelligence.

(For cards outside the US please affix a postage stamp)

BUSINESS REPLY MAIL
FIRST CLASS MAIL   PERMIT NO. 78   WOBURN, MA

POSTAGE WILL BE PAID BY ADDRESSEE

DIRECT MAIL DEPARTMENT
BUTTERWORTH-HEINEMANN
225 WILDWOOD AVE
PO BOX 4500
WOBURN MA 01888-9930

At Butterworth-Heinemann, we are dedicated to providing you with quality service. So that we may keep you informed about titles relevant to your field of interest, please fill in the information below and return this postage-paid reply card. Thank you for your help, and we look forward to hearing from you!

What title have you purchased?

Where was the purchase made?

Name

Job Title

Institution

Address

Town/City

State/County

Zip/Postcode

Country

Telephone

email

☐ Please keep me informed about other books and information services on this and related subjects.

(FOR OFFICE USE ONLY)

BUTTERWORTH-HEINEMANN IS ON THE WEB – http://www.bh.com/

US1

Magazines, newspapers, libraries, trade shows, salespersons, employment interviews, and *on-line information sources* are all sources for overt information collection. Over 90% of intelligence gathering, political and economic, is done through overt sources. See Chapter 2 for more details on open source intelligence and how to protect against it.

Want a tip from someone who's been there? If I were planning an information collection operation against your firm, I would use multiple collection platforms. These would include telephone or room-listening devices, subversion or penetration, trash collection and analysis— always trash. This is called redundancy of collection (i.e., espionage) platforms. It always works.

USE PROVEN COUNTERESPIONAGE STRATEGIES

Here are just a few.

Telephone
The only way to know for sure if your premises are under electronic surveillance (in other words, bugged) is to hire experts for a Technical Surveillance Countermeasures (TSCM) operation—*Call them from a pay phone.* (No, you don't hear clicks if the line is tapped!) You'll know if you get a pro on the other end, because he will give you instructions that sound devious and spooky. If you don't want to heed his advice to the letter, don't hire him.

Here's a sample of what to expect from a person who has had the education, training, and experience to be able to offer a quality counterespionage TSCM sweep. He might have you take a drive along a city street that you rarely use. You may stop at a pay phone you've never used before. You would never use any telephone billed in your name or in your company's name to discuss The Problem with him or his firm.

On the job, you would continue to behave and talk as you previously did. You would tell no one except your corporate security manager about your request for TSCM. The team would arrive unannounced, to be escorted by the corporate security manager to the target area. They would remain therein undisturbed until they tell you otherwise.

The point is, do not discuss proprietary information in a room that contains any type of telephone or intercom. Do not place any computer equipment within three feet of a telephone. Remember that the phone can transmit room conversations even when it's on-hook. And the intercom—especially if it's hardwired into your building wiring—is a transmitter, receiver, and *giant antenna.*

Cellular phones transmit signals that can be eavesdropped on by anyone, from nearly any location between you and the party at the other end. Wireless telephones have identical vulnerability, except over a shorter range of intercept. Don't use either one to discuss anything you don't want a third party to hear. During any telephone conversation in which I participate, except on a secure phone like an STU III with the key turned, I assume that a third party is intercepting the conversation. Most of you couldn't live with that, but maybe you should try.

Fax
It transmits over telephone lines. Do not telecopy any information you can't afford to lose. Better yet, do a quick cost-benefit analysis, then invest in a secure telecopy system.

Computer
Here's a cheap way to get started protecting automated information. Go to your library. Spend the whole day there, reading everything you can find about computer vulnerabilities: LANs, WANs, worms, data diddlers, viruses, Trojan Horses, trap doors, logic bombs, bulletin boards, freeware, shareware, hackers, and the counterculture of perverts like Robert Morris, Jr.; look up the Computer Virus Industry Association and the Computer Security Institute. Then hire a Certified Information Systems Security Professional to give you an objective risk assessment.

Want to read a real life high tech spy story? Read the classic The Cuckoo's Egg by Clifford Stoll (Doubleday: New York, 1989).

Trash

Who's reading your trash—right now, as you read these lines? What would a spy find? Do anther quick cost-benefit analysis, then buy a shredder and use it! Check out the folks who collect your trash—who do they sell it to? And I'll bet some of your key people work at home. Which of your secrets are they giving away in their trash? As a counter-intelligence specialist, I learned how to conduct a trash analysis. Years later, I actually made money at it. I had become a private investigator. The courts have said that trash set upon a public street is public property. Make sure your dumpsters or other trash receptacles are on your property and that your property is clearly marked.

FORECASTING: IS YOUR FIRM A TARGET FOR ESPIONAGE?

Here are five clues to help you figure out the answer to this big question:

1. You're in high technology or biotechnology.
2. Your firm's success is founded on formulas, mixtures, designs, styles, scents, cutting dies, or innovative toys.
3. Your firm manufactures computers or computer parts.
4. You've lost bids by slim margins.
5. Your firm competes in foreign markets.

Obviously, this is not an exclusive list, but if your firm qualifies for any of the Big Five, *it is a target of foreign industrial espionage or competitor intelligence gathering.* I assure you that if you are a corporate officer or senior manager, you are a target, as are your family members and close friends. When I asked the FBI how many companies are targets, they said, "Darn near every company that deals in target activities." When I asked the Defense Investigative Service (DIS) the same question, they said, "A lot—hundreds." Here are just a few additional target positions:

- ◆ Procurement Agent
- ◆ Marketing Manager, VP, or Assistant
- ◆ Budget Analyst
- ◆ Controller
- ◆ Recruiter or Human Resources Executive
- ◆ Engineer or Design Technician

DEFINING ESPIONAGE

It would seem appropriate to define what we're trying to protect ourselves against. In the Industrial Espionage Act of 1996, the Congress defines espionage in seven paragraphs. Here's my synopsis of what Congress said:

> Espionage is the *theft, reproduction, knowing receipt, or destruction of any* proprietary economic information *having a value of not less than $100,000 that is produced for or placed in interstate commerce with the intent to convert it to his or her own benefit.*
>
> Whoever solicits another or conspires with another to commit such offense shall be guilty of the same offense.
>
> Upon conviction of any offense cited above, a human person shall be fined not more than $250,000 or imprisoned not more than fifteen years, or both.
>
> Upon conviction of any offense cited above, a corporation shall be fined not more than $10,000,000.

Proprietary economic information is defined by Congress in three paragraphs. Again, here's a synopsis:

> Proprietary economic information is all forms and types of information, no matter in what form, provided the owner has taken reasonable measures to keep such information confidential, and the information derives independent economic value from not being generally known to, and not being readily ascertainable by legal means by, the public.

The Economic Security Act of 1996 is similar in wording and intent with a few notable exceptions. Section 902 begins, "Engaging in economic espionage to aid foreign nations, governments, corporations, institutions, instrumentalities, or agents . . . " The Security Act installs different penalties for a conviction for espionage: a person will be fined not more than $500,000 or imprisoned not more than 25 years, or both. A corporation will be fined not more than $500,000.

I recommend that you read in their entirety the texts of these landmark documents. To find out how to acquire them, see Appendix B, Resources.

INDICATORS OF ESPIONAGE

You need to be able to recognize when espionage is being conducted against your company. Here are five indicators, provided to me by the chief of a U.S. counterintelligence field office:

1. An inquiry by a stranger about specific projects, new technologies, or developing trade secrets that demonstrates knowledge not released to the public.
2. Competitor knowledge of your negotiating strategies or fallback positions.
3. The appearance of your firm's critical business information in public media or trade publications.
4. The same firm beating you to market with competitive products more than once.
5. One or more people on a special research and development project leaving the company without providing specifics about their new employment.

HOW TO HANDLE THE PROBLEM

Trust your instincts. If you think there's something fishy, chances are, you're right. Call for help right away. If you're a retired counterintelligence agent, don't try to do this yourself. Remember, the lawyer who represents himself has a fool for a client. First call the FBI from a pay phone. You could try the Defense Investigative Service, the Department of Commerce, or even the Financial Crimes Division of your police department. All of these are free. If you have a corporate security executive, he or she will have contacts who will respond promptly.

Call your attorney. Ask her for referrals to credentialed private investigators or security consultants. You're looking for people who have retired from organizations that routinely conduct CI (counterintelligence) or CE (counterespionage) operations. A word of caution: not all special agents of the FBI are experienced, let alone well-trained, in counterespionage. Ask whether they are. Don't assume anything. First, read the next section; then check Appendix B of this book for more resources.

SUPPORT TO PRIVATE INDUSTRY

Numerous U.S. Government agencies routinely provide counterintelligence or counterespionage support to private industry. These include, but are not limited to, the FBI, the Defense Investigative Service (DIS), the Department of Defense Security Institute (DODSI), the Department of Commerce, the Department of State, the Personnel Security Research Institute, the Department of Treasury, and the U.S. Customs Service. Following are just a few examples of the services that some of these agencies can provide.

Support to U.S. industry takes various forms. The FBI's ANSIR program is probably one of the leading education and awareness programs available without charge to American business. The acronym stands for Awareness of National Security Issues and Response. The program is designed to provide unclassified national security threat and warning information to U.S. corporate security directors and executives, law enforcement, and other government agencies. FBI ANSIR coordinators meet regularly with industry leaders and security directors for updates on current national security issues. Each coordinator in the FBI's fifty-six field offices is a member of the American Society for Industrial

Security. This membership enhances public and private sector communication and cooperation for the mutual benefit of both. The Bureau provides information through ANSIR similar to, but in less detail than, that provided in this book.

Since industrial espionage, as of this writing, has been made a Federal crime by the Industrial Espionage Act of 1996, the FBI will investigate. If it finds cause to believe that a violation of U.S. Code Title 18 has taken place (Chapter 37, in particular, pertains to Espionage and Censorship), it may call in additional resources to help you. For example, the Defense Investigative Service, through its Industrial Security and Key Asset Protection Programs, works closely with security managers and facility security officers. DIS offers guidance and training in physical, personnel, information, and automated information security. It provides this support on a company's premises. DIS also provides information about foreign targeting of specific technologies or of specific government contractors.

DODSI develops and presents courses in Department of Defense security countermeasures, security awareness, personnel, physical plant, information, and automation security. DODSI also produces a series of high-quality videos concerning counterespionage techniques.

Customs operates several educational and outreach programs to familiarize private industry with export laws and regulations, and with the roles of the Customs Service in enforcing them. These programs include information regarding foreign intelligence threats to American business as they apply to export issues.

There are two facts to emphasize in this discussion. First, if you're not a government contractor, you probably have never seen a representative of one of these agencies, or you may not have ever heard of some of them or their acronyms. Second, there are more business targets of espionage than can ever be reached by government support. What can you do about these two points? Telephone two or three of the resources cited in this book. Discuss your firm's position, then ask for advice that will make you proactive in counterespionage for your business. (The foregoing information was gathered from the *Annual Report to Congress on Foreign Economic Collection and Industrial Espionage,* July 1995.) Now let's talk further about why you need support.

THE COUNTERESPIONAGE NEEDS
OF PRIVATE INDUSTRY

In June 1995, the National Counterintelligence Center (NACIC) and the U.S. Department of State Overseas Security Advisory Council (OSAC) published a pamphlet entitled *Survey of the Counterintelligence Needs of Private Industry*. The 1994 NACIC-OSAC study sought to ascertain how counterintelligence information is used by private industry and to identify future needs for such information. The survey focused in part on the use and availability of information regarding the threat of espionage.

In December 1994, OSAC mailed 1,400 survey questionnaires to corporate security managers. Only 173 responses were returned. Here follow some of the key details of those responses. (For the sake of brevity, not all questions are reproduced here.)

QUESTION 1:

How frequently does your senior management use threat information about foreign government espionage activities and intentions in making corporate policy decisions?

> Always — 15%
>
> Often — 53%
>
> Seldom — 30%
>
> Never — 2%

This was a baseline question used to discover if senior executives of U.S. corporations are using counterespionage information to make risk management decisions. Apparently, 68% of them do so routinely.

QUESTION 3:

During the past year, has your company expended resources to safeguard against foreign government attacks to your . . .

> Proprietary Information — 66%, Yes
>
> Employees — 62%, Yes

Facilities — 54%, Yes

Telecommunications Systems — 57%, Yes

This question helped to define the willingness of corporate executives to spend money to protect their assets. Apparently, most of them are.

QUESTION 5:

How useful are the following types of information for convincing senior management of the foreign intelligence threat:

Information on the collection methods of foreign governments — 44%

Threats to proprietary information, facilities, employees, and communications systems — 70%

Incidents involving intelligence targeting of other companies — 52%

This was an attempt to ascertain what types of counterintelligence information would be needed by corporate security managers to help them define for senior management the foreign intelligence threat.

QUESTION 6:

Indicate the number of instances you suspect foreign governments have targeted your company during the past year, domestically and overseas.

Suspected domestic instances — 173

Suspected international instances — 273

This provides some insight into the scope of the foreign collection threat as recalled by private industry. In 1994, 74 companies reported 446 incidents. In the majority of these cases, the target was proprietary information. Slightly more than half of the targeting was against U.S. critical technology information.

QUESTION 7:

In those instances where you suspect foreign government targeting of your company, what was targeted?

Proprietary information — 53%

Employees — 18%

Facilities — 8%

Telecommunications systems — 20%

This question identifies those areas of corporate operations or assets believed to be targeted and therefore cause the most concern for the private sector.

Of the 173 U.S. corporations that responded, 68% frequently use threat information about foreign government activities and intentions in making corporate policy decisions. Of the 173 respondents, 67% frequently use counterintelligence information. The biggest users are the financial community (80%) and the industrial/engineering firms (79%).

Finally, the American Society for Industrial Security sponsored a survey called *Technology Theft and Proprietary Protection Assessment* in 1992. The survey revealed that over 50% of attempts to misappropriate proprietary information involve employees or ex-employees. These statistics would seem to reinforce those provided by the National Computer Crime Data Center: current employees account for over 30% of automated information attacks, while former employees account for just under 30% of those attacks.

Given these statistics, it would seem prudent for employers to try to assure the suitability of the people they hire to work with automated information systems. Many of the screening methods used to examine suitability for employment are the same as, or very similar to, those used in a standard background investigation (BI). A thorough background investigation will also reveal behavioral tendencies that are inimical to your company's well-being, such as a criminal record of violence or fraud. In fact, skilled adjudication of a thorough BI may uncover those behavioral patterns that we associate with a proclivity for espionage. We could then conclude that pre-employment screening is both cost-effective and mission-supportive. You'll read about adjudication in greater detail in Chapter 4.

NEW LEGISLATION

On January 25, 1996, Senator William Cohen (R-ME), introduced legislation to amend Title 18 of the U.S. Code to prevent economic espionage and to provide for the protection of U.S. proprietary economic information in interstate and foreign commerce. On February 1, 1996, Senator Herb Kohl (D-WI) introduced the Industrial Espionage Act of 1996 with Senator Arlen Specter (R-PA), and also cosponsored with Specter the Economic Security Act of 1996. The bills passed in both houses.

Senator Cohen's legislation also requires the President to report to Congress on foreign industrial espionage targeted against U.S. industry. (The first *Annual Report to Congress on Foreign Economic Collection and Industrial Espionage* was actually published in July 1995, a year before this requirement was put in place.) The full impact of economic espionage by foreign entities is not known. However, firms that have suffered losses, Cohen claims, reported them in terms of hundreds of millions of dollars, thousands of lost jobs, and irreparable loss of market share.

On the Senate floor, Senator Kohl stated, "It would not be unfair to say that America has become a full-service shopping mall for foreign governments and companies who want to jump-start their business with stolen trade secrets. With expanding technology and a growing global economy, economic espionage is entering its boom years. American companies have estimated that in 1992, they lost $1.8 billion from the theft of their trade secrets."

COUNTERESPIONAGE DEFINED

As you can see from this entire discussion, you need a counterespionage (or counterintelligence) effort. Industrial counterespionage operations detect, evaluate, and neutralize efforts by foreign governments or competitors to steal, alter, or destroy critical business information.

2

What You're Losing— And How to Protect It

THE MOST IMPORTANT ISSUE IN SECURITY IS THREAT

What are you protecting against? If you cannot identify a threat to your assets, you'll waste money on unnecessary protection. For example, if someone steals your computers or your furniture, your insurance will cover it. But consider the liability you would incur if one of your employees or guests were raped or shot on your premises by another employee. What if your trade secrets were compromised? Suppose you were to hire someone who compromised medical or proprietary data entrusted to your care. What would the consequences be?

These management questions are addressed in a risk assessment. To manage your security resources efficiently, you should have a risk assessment completed before you even think about buying alarm systems or guard hours. It will help you isolate your problems and crystallize some cost-effective solutions.

> Security is about solutions to clearly defined problems. It's about increasing productivity. It's about control. It's not about buying hardware or renting guards.

YOUR FIRST 5 STEPS

A risk assessment is an identification and valuation of your assets, a measure of the vulnerabilities of, and threats to, your environment, and an estimate of the cost-effectiveness of safeguards. You will find that a risk assessment is a recurring theme throughout this book. This chapter provides an overview of risk and its management. Equally as important, it includes a list of the technology assets that are being stolen.

Here are the five steps to a risk assessment:

1. Identify and Valuate Assets
2. Analyze Threat
3. Analyze Vulnerabilities
4. Analyze Impact
5. Recommend Improvement Options

STEP 1: IDENTIFY AND VALUATE YOUR ASSETS

If you don't know what you need to protect, or what its value is, you won't be able to assign a realistic budget to loss prevention. For the moment, let's talk about your second most important asset: information. Only about 2% of your firm's information needs to be protected. Here's a list of types of proprietary information to help you figure out what information you need to protect:

First, there's the information you need to operate on a daily basis. This is sensitive information that, if compromised, could cost you time, cash, or material:

◆ Payroll
◆ Accounts Receivable
◆ Accounts Payable
◆ Shipping Schedules
◆ Customer Deadlines

Now think about "CIA"—confidentiality, integrity, and availability of information. If the CIA of these data files were compromised, you'd be hurt, you'd slow down, you might not get paid for awhile, you'd lose some customers, but you'd probably survive. The question of survivability would be determined by the level of acceptable risk to which you could be exposed and still recover. (Acceptable risk is the amount of legal or financial exposure you can underwrite yourself.) This exposure would vary depending on your business, but it's usually a combination of dollars lost, duration of downtime, work hours for recovery, and goodwill. That's why it's part of that 2%.

What People Steal from You

And then there's the information whose confidentiality, integrity, and availability you need for the long-term survival of your business:

◆ Research, Development, and Testing
  ◆ Plans
  ◆ Budget
  ◆ Successes and Failures
◆ Information Related to Employee Turnover
◆ Recruitment Plans
◆ Market Analyses
◆ Plans for Acquisition of Companies or Real Estate
◆ Plans to Acquire New Skills in Your Company
◆ Third-Party Information
  ◆ Received by Your Firm from Another Company
  ◆ Employees' Medical or Background Data

Any compromise of this critical business information would probably expose you to legal consequences or financial disaster, so it's part of that 2%. Let's talk more about your critical business information and how to identify it. You can bet other people have!

More of What People Steal from You

The FBI and the Defense Investigative Service (DIS) have supported segments of U.S. business for years by providing information about foreign espionage threat. Here is some information about the targets of that threat. The following list was validated in June 1996 by the FBI and the Defense Investigative Service (DIS):

Materials
◆ Synthesis and Processing
◆ Electronics and Photonics
◆ Ceramics
◆ Composites
◆ High Performance Metals, Alloys, and Special Coatings

Manufacturing
◆ Flexible Computer-Integrated Manufacturing
◆ Intelligence Processing Equipment
◆ Micro- and Nanofabrication
◆ Systems Management Technologies

Information and Communications
◆ Software
◆ Micro- and Optoelectronics
◆ High Performance Computing and Networking
◆ High-Definition Imaging and Displays
◆ Sensors and Signal Processing
◆ Data Storage and Peripherals
◆ Computer Simulation and Modeling

Biotechnology and Life Sciences
◆ Applied Molecular Biology
◆ Medical Technology

Aeronautics and Surface Transportation
♦ Aeronautics
♦ Surface Transportation Technologies

Energy and Environment
♦ Energy Technologies
♦ Pollution Minimization, Remediation, and Waste Management

And here's a list from another Federal agency:

♦ Abrasive Technologies
♦ Stealth-Related Coatings
♦ Advanced Propulsion Technologies, including slush-hydrogen fuel and torpedo target motors
♦ Aerospace Design Technology
♦ Avionics
♦ Missile Telemetry and Testing Data
♦ Aircraft Communication Systems
♦ Friendly Aircraft Warning Systems (also known as Identification of Friend and Foe, or IFF)
♦ Chemical Finish on Missile Reentry Vehicles

The information categorized above is normally considered under a heading of critical, sensitive, proprietary, or a combination thereof. But there's another category of information that you may need to protect. You should be aware of the role that open source information plays in your business, today, tomorrow, and into the year 2000 and beyond. Let me share with you a portion of the proceedings from *The Fifth International Symposium on Global Security and Global Competitiveness: Open Source Solutions*. It was held September 15 to 18, 1996, at the Sheraton Premiere in Tysons Corner, Virginia, and hosted by Robert Steele.

According to quotes attributed by Steele to Lt. Gen. C. Norman Wood, 90% of the information that the U.S. military could have used to our military advantage in Desert Shield and Desert Storm was available from open sources—most of that from the press, and some from historical data that was still valid. The historical data, for example, included the Iraqi order of battle or style of fighting. CNN, Reuters, and other news services were providing timely, accurate information that was discounted by senior U.S. officials because it wasn't classified, that is, it wasn't coming from intelligence sources.

Open source information will play a larger role in government and corporate decision-making into the twenty-first century. It is cheaper, easier to verify, and easier to use than classified information. It also doesn't encourage the creation of fiefdoms of knowledge hoarding, as classified information frequently does.

Knowledge hoarding occurs when people believe that they are perceived as powerful or in control because of their possession of classified information. They leak tidbits, intimating that they alone are privy to or can get the desired information. Field commanders who served in Operation Desert Storm complain bitterly, if privately, that this occurred with startling regularity in that conflict. That is why they struck bargains with CNN. The line commanders of combat units covertly allowed CNN reporters to go on missions that had been placed off-limits to them, in return for the intelligence being gathered by CNN field reporters.

I personally experienced the effects of knowledge hoarding in Europe when I was a counterintelligence specialist handling terrorist threat analysis. Senior U.S. Army Headquarters in Europe, in possession of terrorist threat reports provided by the Department of State, the Central Intelligence Agency, and the Defense Intelligence Agency, declined to pass on those reports to the commanders in the field. They told the commanders that the reports were "highly classified" and that the commanders had no need to know. There is no such thing as "highly classified." There are only three levels of classification: confidential, secret, and top secret. And I can assure you that those terrorist threat reports sent to the Army headquarters elements were no higher than secret. Further, the commanders of the soldiers whose lives depended on early, accurate warning of terrorist activity certainly had a need to know the information.

If you seek to find any logic in this charade, you will fail. There is nothing logical (or professionally ethical) about failing to provide information to the people who need it.

Mortimer B. Zuckerman, the owner of *U.S. News & World Report* and the keynote speaker at the International Symposium on Global

Security and Global Competitiveness, likewise observed that the national security establishment must wean itself away from classified information as the primary source of strength and knowledge. A capitalist society uses open source information to build industry and commerce. A government needs to get in step and acknowledge open sources as the most valuable source of information about who's doing what to whom.

Paul Strassman, former Director of Defense Information and former Chief Information Officer (CIO) at Xerox, observed that there is an Economic Value Added (EVA) by any private enterprise that acknowledges the value of Knowledge Capital. I interpreted his definition of knowledge capital to be those human and nonhuman sources of information and expertise that exist within an enterprise and that are within its reach outside the company itself. For example, those companies with a sales staff make every sales call a social relationship. The salesperson gleans competitor information from the encounter (probably the simplest form of competitor intelligence) and eventually asks the contact person for a favor (here's an example of recruitment in espionage). The salesperson contributes to her employer the knowledge she has gained from the relationship, as well as the value of having a person "on the inside" in the form of her sales contact.

Strassman cited a study that he had been commissioned to do in 1994. He noted the top ten industrial sectors that applied the concept of EVA, including: Beverages; Drugs & Research; Tobacco; Food Processing; Medical Products; and Personal Care. He asserted that 79.9% of the companies studied spent more on acquisition and use of information than on capital assets. Banks and other financial institutions spend over 86% on acquisition and use of information. As an example, he asserted that capital and management costs for 770 of the largest U.S. firms amounted to Financial ($16,840 per person, per year) and Information Management ($35,000 per person, per year) in 1994. With regard to actual industrial espionage, he quipped, "Never suspect conspiracy where incompetence will explain what happened."

Edward F. Dandar, Jr., Office of the Deputy Assistant Secretary of Defense for Intelligence and Security (Intelligence Systems Support Office), offered the following observations in regard to the Global Information Environment:

An adequate computer infrastructure to tie intelligence analysts into open source information does not appear to exist. In the view of the Commission [on the Roles and Capabilities of the United States Intelligence Community], the creation of such an infrastructure should be a top priority of the Director for Central Intelligence and a top priority for funding. With more and more [open source] information available by electronic means, its usefulness in intelligence analysis can only grow. The intelligence community must be able to obtain information from a wide variety of sources on a continuous basis in order to satisfy the needs of decision-makers. The intelligence analyst does not have the time, expertise, or training to continuously and exhaustively collect information on multiple targets. The need, then, is for an integrated information environment where analysts can seamlessly exploit information repositories and expert knowledge.

The first task in satisfying the information needs of decision-makers is to ascertain what relevant information may be on public record. The next two steps are to determine the most cost-effective approach to mining the right sources, and to recover the information in a timely manner. These tasks are becoming increasingly difficult as the volume and diversity of information grow. Adding to the difficulty is the fact that government researchers and analysts typically do not hold membership in those professional organizations in the private sector that are dedicated to information research.

The private sector members have the education, expertise, and willingness necessary to help each other. They network and attend professional symposia, conventions, and trade shows to keep abreast of new developments in open source information. These information professionals have domestic and international networks of academic and professional contacts that can be leveraged. Most importantly, the members of these professional organizations are driven by the bottom line: they earn a living being very good at what they do.

These professionals earn a living by examining large volumes of disparate information to glean a few nuggets of relevance and importance to their paying clients. They have the ability to work within fragmented systems that have disparate connections to collate, analyze, and report business or technical intelligence clearly and concisely.

This ability will be recognized as the mandate of the U.S. Intelligence Community. The Community's ability to accomplish this mandate in the year 2000 will be limited by the difficulties in transforming organizations and people from the old way of doing business to the new way.

The old way includes little else beside exploiting classified sources. The new way involves, for example, having the Intelligence Community Open Source Program Office commission a vendor to explore the Internet as a resource for open source information (OSI) pertaining to Africa and Latin America (as was done in 1995). Another new approach is to develop OSI pilot projects to establish directories of government, industry, academia, and other private subject matter experts, which was underway for 1996 to 1997.

STEP 2: IDENTIFY AND ANALYZE THE THREAT TO YOUR BUSINESS— *WHO'S STEALING FROM YOU*

Fire, flood, earthquake, explosion, strikes, theft, and electrical blackouts all constitute types of threat. Insurance takes care of most of these threats. But what about threat to information? You can't buy insurance to protect your critical business information. Do you have any idea who would steal your information, or corrupt it? Who violates the CIA (confidentiality, integrity, and availability) of your critical and sensitive business information? The list is short but deadly:

♦ Foreign Governments on Behalf of Their Industries
♦ American Competitors
♦ Current Employees
♦ Former Employees

STEP 3: IDENTIFY AND ANALYZE THE VULNERABILITIES OF YOUR BUSINESS

The Webster dictionary states that *vulnerable* means *capable of being wounded*, or *open to attack*. I would like to broaden Webster's horizons by adding, *capable of being exposed to risk*, or *exposure to risk*. I use the concept of risk management in the practice of loss prevention. Risk is the chance of injury, damage, or loss, as well as the degree of probability of loss.

Say you hire a person without a background check. He has a criminal record of convictions for violent behavior. You've just made your employees and your visitors vulnerable to him. You've made your business vulnerable to the criminal (and legal) consequences of negligent hiring. Stockholders would be vulnerable to tort consequences if this new hire shoots someone on your premises.

What if you hire another person without a background check. He's just plain unsuitable. He really was not a data entry clerk on the three jobs he held during the last fifteen months. As one previous employer put it: "He was always into lottsa stuff." Now he's into your information systems.

It Can Happen to Your Company

The American Society for Industrial Security (ASIS) has sponsored three surveys to uncover firsthand information regarding industrial espionage and theft of intellectual property. Here is some information from the survey done in 1995:

♦ Intellectual property theft from American business rose over 300% during the period of 1993 to 1995.
♦ Potential losses to Corporate America resulting from theft of intellectual property are about $24 billion annually.
♦ Reported losses of intellectual property rose from 9.9 per month in 1992 to 32 per month in 1995—an increase of 323%.
♦ 60% of the financial losses resulted from theft of strategic plans, R&D, and manufacturing process information.
♦ The top five countries involved in theft of intellectual property from U.S. companies were China, Canada, France, India, and Japan.
♦ *75% of all incidents involved employees working in a position of trust.*

STEP 4: ANALYZE IMPACT

In business terms, this means that you look at the consequences of your exposure to risk under two conditions: with protection and without protection. For example, could the lack of an applicant screening program adversely affect profit? How much more profit would you retain by paying for background screening? Then you consider the cost of maintaining your acceptable level of risk. You go through these steps for each type of asset, each threat, each vulnerability. This is your cost-benefit analysis.

STEP 5: IDENTIFY IMPROVEMENT OPTIONS

These options should have become apparent as you proceeded through step four, the Impact Analysis. Since impact analyses address asset identifications, threat analyses, and vulnerability analyses, review them as you begin to examine options for loss prevention. Just remember, these are not the Ten Commandments. They are guidelines for protecting your assets. Later in this book, you will learn how to apply this knowledge to a simple technique for assessing risk. This assessment will be methodical and objective; its products will be measurable.

PROGRAMMATIC CONSIDERATIONS

Your Loss Prevention Program, like all business programs, must be evaluated periodically. This is usually done through a security consult, which is an evaluative process. The process may be used to answer various questions for your management team, such as:

♦ Is the program accomplishing the desired goals?
♦ Can the same goals be accomplished at a lower cost?
♦ Can more goals be accomplished at the same cost?
♦ Can the program be improved?
♦ Is the program necessary?

The goals, of course, must be reasonable, specific, and measurable. For example:

♦ *Reduce loss* from $18,000 per year to under $5,000 per year from forced entry into the warehouse.
♦ Verify all specified critical information on every employment application within ten days after hire.

A cost-benefit analysis will then help your management team move from evaluation to budgeting. Together, you and the consultants will:

♦ Identify loss-prevention alternatives for increasing productivity
♦ Estimate costs for each alternative (capital, noncapital, direct, and support)
♦ Demonstrate the benefits of each alternative
♦ Compare the costs and benefits

The Bottom Line

Here are some benefits from the evaluation:

♦ Clarification of liability issues
♦ Wider range of options
♦ Rational analysis brought into decision-making
♦ Valuation of future consequences
♦ More efficient utilization of resources

3

Operations Security: Counterespionage behind the Scenes

Operations security (OPSEC) is the process of protecting critical business information by concealing or changing indicators that disclose that information. It evolves from a risk assessment. Its scope depends on, and is guided by, each element of the risk assessment. OPSEC is the cost-effective way to protect proprietary economic information.

The terms critical business information, proprietary economic information, trade secrets, sensitive information, and critical information are used interchangeably in this book. The terms all mean

> all forms and types of financial, business, scientific, technical, economic, or engineering information, including data, plans, tools, mechanisms, compounds, formulas, designs, prototypes, processes, procedures, programs, codes, or commercial strategies, whether tangible or intangible, and however stored, compiled, or memorialized, if the owner has taken reasonable measures to keep such information confidential; and the information derives independent economic value, actual or potential, from not being generally known to, and not being readily ascertainable, acquired, or developed by legal means by the public. (Economic Security Act of 1996)

Risk assessment is the process of evaluating assets, identifying threat, vulnerability, and consequences of failure to protect those assets;

and recommending improvements to prevent loss. You'll remember from Chapter 2 that a risk assessment is expressed in five steps:

1. Identification and valuation of assets
2. Identification of threat
3. Evaluation of vulnerabilities
4. Analysis of impact (cost-benefit analysis)
5. Improvement options

HERE'S HOW IT WORKS IN REAL LIFE

It is essential that you associate a value with each asset, for when you arrive at steps 4 and 5, you'll need to have a basis for comparison of cost. You'll need to compare the impact of losing the asset with the impact of spending a given sum of money to protect it. Since OPSEC is based on the paradigm of risk assessment, you will buy only the protection that you need (this is the Security Manager's Rule of Parsimony). The paradigm asserts that if there is no threat, there is no vulnerability. On the other hand, once a threat is matched to a vulnerable asset, that asset may be found to be exposed to other threats. To protect your assets, you need a program of loss prevention that consists of counterespionage, OPSEC, and security.

Security, as I use it in this book, consists of those physical activities on your premises whose purpose is to deter, delay, detect, and report loss-inducing behavior. This behavior could be breaking and entering; it could be an unsuitable person seeking employment; or it could be an information leak. All of these are threats to your assets.

Counterespionage or counterintelligence (CE or CI) activities identify threat to specified information assets. When your CI special agent (SA) reports a threat to you, she will place it in context with a vulnerability. Here's how an intelligence spot report might read, when reported by a CI agent in the field.

Chinese HUMINT handlers have targeted your plant in South Butte, Arkansas for collection of technical intelligence concerning a radar system for automobiles. They have placed young American women of Chinese descent, with relatives in China, in Cactus Butte, the bar next to your assembly plant. The women serve both lunch and dinner. They are aggressive in engaging young, single, male plant workers in conversation about the work in the plant. The questions usually focus on the design of the micro-ROM2000. This breakthrough technology is reported to be the only system under development that can be fitted to any automobile manufactured in the United States. It is reported as three to five months away from its first scheduled field testing. That testing is to be in the controller for the Luxo XRL automobile radar system.

 This reporting SA sat in Cactus Butte during three lunch periods and one dinner hour. The preceding information concerning the micro-ROM2000 was overheard only during those encounters. The SA did not attempt to elicit anyone for any information.

This spot report was a "data dump" of everything that the CI agent overheard your workers talk about in that bar. If time permitted, she would have consulted an OPSEC technician specializing in the target's electronics. She could then provide you with an analysis of what she deduced about your trade secret. This scenario is what's called a bar watch. You can understand why it's cheap, effective, and often used near target sites.

 In this spot report, counterintelligence answered Who? What? When? Where? and How? I think we already know why: we're working with breakthrough technology on that micro-ROM. We also know that we have at least a HUMINT problem.

 However, an experienced CI agent would tell you that chances are, we have a SIGINT problem as well. Signal intelligence collects information from intercepted wire and wireless communications. If I were handling this collection operation, I would have a list of all telephone numbers assigned to the target plant, along with matching *keyword* lists. (More on keywords in a moment.) Thus, I would expect a given group of telephone numbers at the plant, assigned to engineering, to yield conversations about "tech intel," or technical intelligence. I would have those numbers monitored during working hours. I would also expect these same engineers, or their spouses, to talk about their jobs over their home telephones.

HERE'S HOW SIGNAL INTELLIGENCE IS GATHERED

Keywords are words or phrases generated by special intelligence collection requirements (SICR). A SICR concerning the micro-ROM2000 to be used in the Luxo XRL automobile would include the phrase *ROM2000*, the phrase *Luxo XRL*, and the words *automobile* and *radar*. It would include technical terms, and probably the phrase *Site R* (you'll see why in a minute). The keywords are managed by the case officer who ensures that they are protected by the agent in charge of the surreptitious listening post.

In the early stages of an operation, the keyword list is used to fish for information. The list is synchronized by computer with the listening system for a given block of telephone numbers. While all telephone conversations may be intercepted, only those that contain keywords are captured on tape. When someone articulates phrases from the keyword list, the voice intercept system starts the recording system. Recording will continue until a dial tone occurs, or until an intercept analyst turns off the recorder.

The telephone numbers of origin and the dialed telephone numbers will be identified and tentatively associated with the keywords. When association is confirmed, the intercept team will purge from the system those numbers that were not fruitful. The remaining numbers, those carrying conversations relevant to a mission, are reassigned to an automatic recording system. Thereafter, each call originating from or placed to the numbers on which keywords were heard will be recorded. In the next step, the telephone numbers are associated with people. When names are confirmed, these people are listed as potential targets for HUMINT. They are identified as knowledgeable and available for HUMINT collection against current SICR.

Life is a lot easier for the voice intercept analysts when they have organization directories and telephone books. Don't make life easier for the people who are threatening your livelihood; don't give out charts, reports, or directories to strangers. Remember what your Mom told you: be careful of friendly strangers.

If I were leading this operation, we would be listening through both HUMINT and SIGINT platforms for other information as well.

While such information would not yield trade secrets, it would provide tips on how we could more easily acquire trade secrets, and who the most likely targets would be. It would work like this.

Let's say the engineers who design updates of the ROM2000 make plans by telephone to begin traveling in a company van each Thursday afternoon to a private suite in a hotel forty miles away. The agents I've recruited will now report OPSEC *patterns. The HUMINT platforms will be used to validate the raw information gathered by the SIGINT analysts; this is now usable intelligence.*

In this case, for example, telephone conversations and local observations reveal a *routine assembly of personnel with special skills that are uniquely applicable to a specific piece of intelligence* that we need. *Advance reservations* at the hotel, for the next three months; *reservations in the hotel restaurant,* and travel of *key executives* from the plant to the Thursday evening dinners—eighty miles round trip, just for dinner. These activities constitute a pattern, indicators that can lead to disclosure of proprietary information.

Now we bug the van, we bug the hotel suite, and we insert one or two locally recruited sources into that hotel to serve and ingratiate themselves to the engineers. And yes, we bug the homes of those engineers and key executives who travel to the hotel each week. (In the real scenario of this case, the CI agent learned that the hotel was a few minutes' drive from our client's remote research site, called Site R in this story.)

If the stakes were high enough, I would order some compromise probes. I would probe a few members of the group with sex, alcohol, and illicit drugs. My local sources would try to separate two or three men from the rest of the group and get these men to spend the weekend with them, doing sex and taking drugs on videotape.

LOSS PREVENTION PROGRAM DEVELOPMENT

The preceding was the actual reasoning of a counterintelligence agent tailoring an OPSEC program to protect a special project in 1995. Take a look at Figure 3.1. It shows you how counterespionage, OPSEC, and security work together. The project objectives in the figure are similar to the real thing, except for a name change. And in the real project, Loss

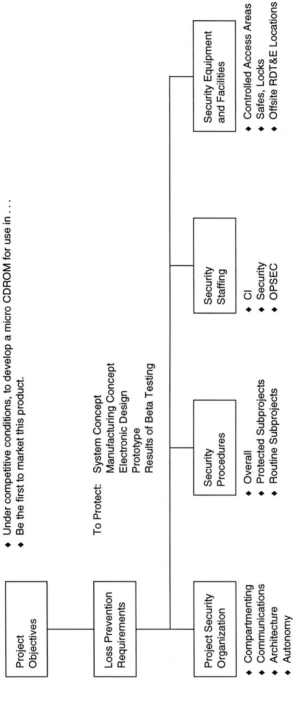

Project ROM2000
Loss Prevention Program Development

Project Objectives
- Under competitive conditions, to develop a micro CDROM for use in ...
- Be the first to market this product.

Loss Prevention Requirements

To Protect: System Concept
              Manufacturing Concept
              Electronic Design
              Prototype
              Results of Beta Testing

Project Security Organization
- Compartmenting
- Communications
- Architecture
- Autonomy

Security Procedures
- Overall
- Protected Subprojects
- Routine Subprojects

Security Staffing
- CI
- Security
- OPSEC

Security Equipment and Facilities
- Controlled Access Areas
- Safes, Locks
- Offsite RDT&E Locations

Project Managers define their own objectives and then share this information with the loss prevention manager. The LP manager and the PMs then decide what needs to be protected. Anything that *needs* protection becomes an LP requirement, and earns a place on the project LP budget.

Figure 3.1   Project ROM2000: Loss Prevention Program Development

Prevention Requirements numbered fifteen. Also, we tried in vain to kill the idea about off-site RDT&E (Research, Development, Test, and Evaluation) locations. Let's talk about the rest of Figure 3.1 for a few minutes.

Project Security Organization

"Compartmenting" refers to segregating information into portions that are made available only to people who have a need to know the details in that compartment or work unit. Communication is the foundation of relationships. In order to have a cohesive group of dedicated LP (loss prevention) specialists, your members must understand that all channels are open, all the time. For example, it's alright to disagree about which types of telephones and two-way radios the LP staff will use. Form follows function; therefore, it may become necessary to modify the architecture of the LP Telecommunications Program. If human communications have been effective, the group will be cohesive, and no one is going to wince about losing turf or acquiring new responsibilities over a telephone system. Autonomy bespeaks empowerment. As long as the LP staff and its clients understand the implications of using each type of electronic communications, any LP staff member can make a decision that binds the entire staff. That may not be the same decision that other members would have made, and that's okay. Each member is the product of his or her education and training, so if another person suggests a different approach, try it. Chances are, your Telecommunications Program will be enhanced.

Security Procedures

Everybody must agree to enforce the Project Security Operating Procedures, once the client signs the security policy. However, there may be subprojects that need special care and attention. Each must be handled separately, respecting the compartmentalizations. Equal care must be paid not to expend resources to protect routine subprojects "just in case." You have OPSEC specialists whose job it is to constantly surveil the entire operation. They will let you know about potential new vulnerabilities.

Security Staffing

Counterintelligence is tasked with identifying, characterizing, and neutralizing threat. In this project, CI would have to identify other companies that could reasonably be expected to profit from knowledge of the information designated for protection. Characterization would include briefly citing their current state of tools, dies, engineering talent, suitability of premises, financial resources, financial encumbrances, and so forth. It should be clear from this that your CI specialists must be intimate with the structure and function of your firm, as well as with the project being considered. Operations security protects critical information from defined threat. It protects by first examining friendly operations through the eyes of the enemy, searching for vulnerabilities, and probing for tidbits of information revealed by stereotyped activities. (You'll read more about stereotypical activities shortly, when we get to the OPSEC Evaluation Report.) Once the OPSEC team sees opportunities for exploitation, it begins to conceal those exploitable weaknesses. The security team gathers all the analyses from the CI and OPSEC specialists and designs protection platforms for the vulnerable information. This may range from requiring that certain documents be kept in a safe or under direct personal control, to frequently changing off-site meeting places and patterns of behavior.

Security Equipment and Facilities

The most effective communications will foster group cohesiveness. Cohesive groups need only occasional reminders and straightforward guidance to stay out of restricted areas. Controlled access and safes, locks, alarms, guards, and dogs may be necessary, but should be resorted to only as a last resort.

BACK TO THE MISSION

At this point, if you had the luxury of having counterespionage agents, OPSEC specialists, and a security staff in your firm, they would meet and unanimously agree to one thing: They must conduct an OPSEC Evaluation of your Project ROM2000. Look at Figure 3.2. As you follow the outline with me, remember that this is not a dummy document. The OER (OPSEC Evaluation Report) and the Risk Assessment constitute the two most important tools in CI strategy. Indeed, the OER is called a living or dynamic document; that's because the threat and vulnerabilities may change by the time your first CI strategy has been implemented.

Outline for OPSEC Evaluation Report

1. Introduction

    A. Objectives

        1. To protect the following assets at Site R:

            * System Concept
            * Manufacturing Concept
            * Results of Beta Testing

        2. To protect the following assets at Headquarters:

            * Electronic Design
            * Prototype

    B. Special Instructions. Site R has had ongoing projects, not associated with this one, that conduct R&D in cutting edge technology.

    C. Scope

        1. Physical Security
        2. Information Security
        3. Personnel Security
        4. Special aspects

2. Threat. Only specific, identified threats are cited in this report. Normally, Threat becomes a separate annex or appendix, and is a copy of the CI agent's report(s).

    A. HUMINT
    B SIGINT
    C. Terrorism(?)

3. Vulnerabilities and Recommendations: Vulnerabilities are prioritized as budget line items, along with their demonstrated threat. The threat may be synopsized, or references may be cited:

    A. Vulnerability: Employees talk freely in public about their work at Site R

        1. Threat: HUMINT agents are in place at Cactus Butte bar.

        2. Impact: During the next five months, the System Concept may be compromised, costing us $1.2 million in direct expense, plus product lead time, plus the sacrifice of leading edge technology to a foreign competitor, in violation of Federal law.

        3. Recommendations: Assign one security specialist to work full time at Site R. Have her security-brief every employee and executive who works at or visits the site or the hotel close to it. Consider counterintelligence monitoring of Cactus Butte, and vary the schedule for visiting the hotel and the site. Have Security manage the scheduling. Estimated additional cost for next quarter: $2,500.

    B. Vulnerability:

        1. Threat
        2. Impact
        3. Recommendations

Figure 3.2   Outline for OPSEC Evaluation Report

Notice first how the LP Program (Figure 3.1) provides input to the OER. It gives direction to the document that will eventually serve as a counterespionage strategy document, the guide for an OPSEC plan, and classification guidance for the security department. Let me talk just briefly about this last topic.

If you look again at the LP Program Development sheet, you'll notice the phrase, "Under competitive conditions." That is the signal that the Vice President of Marketing gives to the Corporate Director of Security (also known as the Loss Prevention Manager). It is the red flare designating a hot landing zone. It says, *We know that the United States Department of Commerce has placed this technology under close hold; it must not be released outside the United States. We know that it could revolutionize the auto industry overseas; it could destroy the U.S. auto industry because foreign industry could produce the technology at a fraction of the cost. We must protect this technology, beginning with the hand-scribbled notes from the systems people.* Now you know why the first item under Project Security Organization is Compartmenting: a close hold must be exercised over this information.

Now look at where it says "To Protect." The LP staff has its mission statement right there. The LP staff engineers and other program members have an obligation to share information with the broadest possible segment of knowledgeable staff. This must happen in order that nothing be overlooked in the early phases, possibly negating thousands of hours of work. But this sharing of information must be done with restraint. Refer again to the discussion about the Industrial Espionage Act of 1996 at the beginning of this chapter; it gives you some clues about how to handle restraints on the use of trade secrets:

> All forms and types of information, no matter in what form, provided the owner has taken reasonable measures to keep such information confidential, and the information derives independent economic value from not being generally known to, and not being readily ascertainable by legal means by the public.

Your engineers are going to share that information with the widest possible audience, unless you place restraints on the information in a timely, concise manner. Those restraints are: (1) take reasonable measures to keep the information confidential; (2) inform the authorized holders of that information that it is confidential; and (3) show them that there is one prescribed way to protect it. Obviously, the security office must demonstrate the prescribed method of protection and ensure that the staff respects that prescription. Thus, classification guides set forth the proper marking (e.g., company confidential, proprietary, etc.) and the manner in which each type of document must be protected. I think you will agree that no matter what protective marking you affix to the documents containing your critical information, you do not want your employees discussing it in the Cactus Butte bar. Now back to the OER (OPSEC Evaluation Report).

Look under 1. B., Special Instructions. It reports that your technical staff has been using Site R for RDT&E of secret technology for a long time. This is a most important fact, for we now assume that the entire town is aware of the mission of Site R. In addition, your company is sending the people who work on the ROM2000 at headquarters to Site R for a couple of days every week. We assume that the entire town knows this fact as well, based on these repeated, similar activities, or stereotypical activities. We now deduce that your company has painted a come-hither sign on its ROM2000 proprietary information. What to do about it?

There is no easy answer here. I will tell you what we did for this particular client, but you will have to carefully examine your own situation to ensure that the improvement options will work in the environment under your care. Our first concern was whether the client had taken any preventive measures at all before launching the program. He had taken none. So we used deception, or "black propaganda" to mislead competitors. It worked like this. The client's LP manager brought in a security manager from a distant company and gave him a role to play. His role was that of an acquisitions manager for a multinational electronics company. He leaked to the Cactus Butte crowd intimations that the senior executives and design engineers were meeting with him at Site R to avoid panic among the employees at headquarters. Their company (our client) was to participate in a losing merger with his multinational electronics firm. It would have been a great OPSEC maneuver, except that the outside man got a little too exuberant: he actually *named a foreign company* as the winner in the putative merger.

By the way, some would call this an Offensive Counterintelligence Operation, or OFCO. It must be planned by people with special training and field experience. It makes extensive use of tradecraft specialties, including deception, defensive source operations (DSO), the turning and handling of hostile agents, and remote electronic surveillance. It is an offensive operation designed to aggressively neutralize hostile intelligence collection activities. It works for foreign governments, foreign industry, and competing American companies. I am not going to tell you how to undertake an OFCO or a DSO. That would be as ethical as teaching you how to make booby traps. If your firm ever needs an OFCO or a DSO for survival, call the experts. Be prepared to pay a small fortune. If they seem prepared to negotiate price, walk away. Look at it this way; if you believe that you have found the best of the best for this mission, why would you expect him to lower his price? Does that mean his expertise is not worth what he asked for originally? One more thing. You may feel inclined to "sit in" on or participate in their operations. If they agree to this, fire them. Then get a team that will not compromise you and your company by letting you know what the team is doing.

REALITY CHECK

If you still doubt the threat of foreign industrial espionage, remember that industrial espionage is driven by money. That's the bottom line. As the *President's 1996 Annual Report to Congress on Foreign Collection and Industrial Espionage* asserts, this business is going to cost Americans billions by the millennium—and, in turn, reap billions for foreign powers who will have spent thousands. That's an enviable return on investment. There are countries whose very survival relies on surreptitious theft of American technology. Think about our friends, France, Israel, China, and Russia. Then consider our friends India and Pakistan, at war with each other, and Iran and Iraq, likewise at war.

Also consider domestic espionage, or Americans stealing from Americans. Think about cereal boxes. That's right—cereals. You probably didn't know that the cereal-packaging people, the ones who design those crazy-looking wrappings for little crunchies, have some of the finest counterespionage staffs in the world. They have to. Because their competitors have the finest industrial spies in the world. And the toy companies play the same cloak and dagger game.

THE EYES OF THE ENEMY

By now you will have perceived that the most astute OPSEC practition-ers have been taught the intricacies of espionage. That is why they are so good at divining what the other guy is thinking and planning; they are former spies. They can size up an operation and pick out the indi-cators that will make your company vulnerable to a hostile collection effort—that's the counterespionage jargon for espionage.

By the same token, they do not waste time and resources on trivia. They always consider the elements of vulnerability. Look at Figure 3.3. Notice the five factors that make a piece of information vulnerable: Vis-ibility, Utility, Perishability, Exploitability, and Protectability.

REACH OUT AND TOUCH SOMEONE . . . WITH AN OER

Let's not forget about your most precious asset: people. They protect your second most precious asset: information. What if one of your em-ployees is a spy? How would you know? Since you're doing an OER anyway, let's take a moment to look at vulnerabilities in your personnel system. I recently had a conversation with an Army Counterintelligence Special Agent who reminded me of a case that was relevant to this issue.

There was a young man, stationed at Fort Bragg, North Carolina, who had been noticed by his peers to be constantly living beyond his means. He had paid cash for a new Corvette as well as for a fur coat for his wife. He and his wife had taken frequent trips to Mexico City and to Vienna, Austria. At least two co-workers had noticed him photocopying documents containing classified information to which he should not have had access. And no one had said a word for two years. One day, a routine review of photographs of people entering and leaving a Soviet Embassy outside the United States caused some alarm among the Fed-eral agents in attendance. One of them realized that he had seen this guy, in another set of photographs, coming out of the Soviet Embassy in Washington, D.C.

After this man was arrested, he admitted in an interview with Fed-eral counterspies that he had been selling intelligence-related documents

---

The Five Factors of Vulnerability

1. *Visibility* (or detectability)

   a. What is the probability that espionage agents or competitor intelligence agents will be made aware of the information?

   b. What is the probability that those agents could access the information?

2. *Utility*

   a. What is the probability that the information will be perceived by agents as useful to their employers?

   b. Would it satisfy published requirements of a foreign intelligence service?

   c. Would it satisfy a competitor's requirements?

3. *Perishability*

   a. Is there a date beyond which the information will no longer be useful to the competitor?

   b. Can the espionage agent verify and transmit the information before that date?

4. *Exploitability*

   a. Can the competitor respond to the information in time, and in a manner detrimental to the owner of the information?

   b. Would additional information be necessary in order for the competitor to exploit the original information to his advantage, and to the detriment of the owner?

5. *Protectability*

   a. Do you have a written policy for protecting trade secrets and proprietary information?

   b. Do you limit dissemination of the information to a few persons who need to know?

   c. Have those persons signed noncompete agreements?

Figure 3.3   The Five Factors of Vulnerability

for nearly two years. Why? It was lucrative. It was exciting. More significantly for the purposes of personnel security, he said that his employer, the United States Army, would not promote him, so he was angry and wanted revenge. Anger, revenge, and greed are the emotions most often found to be precursors of traitorous behavior.

In private industry, there is nearly always a set of indicators that would allow management to identify a person who perceives management as hostile. The management team who is alert to the indicators will react before the person exacts revenge for his anger, through theft, violence, or industrial espionage. Here are additional factors that can lead to distress in the workplace:

+ Relocation
+ Reorganization of the work force
+ Feuding among managers
+ Sexual harassment
+ Discrimination

You may have realized by now that OPSEC deals with risk—the exposure to harm. We can say that risk management balances risk against objectives or mission. The profitability of any mission is directly related to protecting its assets. The most important assets are people and information. Since you cannot protect every asset from every threat all of the time, you need to strike a balance. That balance is achieved by using the systematic method of the five-step risk analysis. Let's explore a few more practical applications of the OPSEC process before we close the chapter.

HOW TO COVER YOUR ASSETS

Shred *all* your paper waste. It is not cost-effective for an agent or an analyst to sift through shredded sandwich bags, newspapers, and your weekly newsletters looking for tidbits of secrets. Another benefit to shredding everything is bulk. If at all possible, have your shredded waste picked up only once a week. Tell the waste company that you will call them when you are ready for a pickup. Yes, it is more expensive this way, but that is why you do a cost analysis of each improvement option in step 5 of the risk assessment. Also, consider outsourcing your shredding. Again, a benefit-cost analysis is in order.

Maintain low predictability. If you have been sending technicians and executives to a certain hotel each time they need to discuss critical information about a new project, you can bet that your assets are at risk. Related to this is the necessity for avoiding an unusual pattern of behavior, a stereotypical activity that is exclusive to a particular endeavor. One example might be opening the west wing of your building only when a secret project is scheduled. To avoid drawing attention to special projects, leave the wing open all the time. The employees will figure out a use for it.

Screen all your applicants, all the time. Employment applicants are especially dangerous when you are in dire need of whatever they offer. That nearly-perfect engineer who seems to have all the answers and who asks all the right questions may be on an espionage mission, or conducting an offensive counterintelligence operation against you.

Maintain high awareness. Be aware that discreet pieces of information can be brought together in what the OPSEC analyst calls a mosaic to form a refined intelligence product. Here are sources of information about your company that you must monitor carefully:

♦ Vendors and Suppliers
♦ Copyrights and Patents
♦ Licenses
♦ Brokerage Reports
♦ Joint Venture Proposals and Agreements
♦ Annual Reports
♦ Prospectus and Brochures
♦ Conferences, Trade Shows, and Symposia
♦ Banking Relationships

The next chapter will take you into the details of personnel security. It will explain why spies spy and, for the first time in print, how spies recruit your employees.

4

How to Protect Your People

Earlier, I wrote about the cost-effectiveness of preemployment screening. In Chapter 1, I mentioned that it not only verifies a potential employee's suitability, but may also reveal an applicant's history of violent behavior. In the following cases, no preemployment screening or criminal record checks were performed. In the wording of the courts, "*But for the employers' failure to perform a duly diligent background check,*" the rapes and theft would not have occurred. There is no question that background checks are invaluable for foreseeing and avoiding violence and theft. You will read shortly how useful they are in preventing industrial espionage.

WOMAN RAPED, SUES FOR $2 MILLION: EMPLOYER FAILED TO CHECK EMPLOYEE'S CRIMINAL RECORD

A tenant of a housing authority was raped in her townhouse by a housing inspector employed by the authority. The inspector had been convicted previously for robbery and assault; at the time of his hiring, two months before the assault on the tenant, he had been under indictment for rape. The tenant sued for negligent hiring, claiming the authority failed to ascertain if the inspector was trustworthy, and did not make a reasonable inquiry to determine his fitness for his job. [Cramer v. Housing Opportunities Commission, 304 Md. 705, 501 A.2d 35 (1985)]

EMPLOYER SUBJECT TO LIABILITY
FOR HIRING CLERK CONVICTED OF RAPE
AND ROBBERY

A secretary was assaulted and murdered by a mail room clerk who worked in the same company. He was convicted of murder. He had been convicted of rape and robbery before being hired. The parents of the secretary sued the employer for negligent hiring. The court held that where the plaintiffs alleged that the employer knew or should have known of an employee's dangerous proclivities, the employer may be liable for negligent hiring if the employer's negligence was the proximate cause of the injury and was foreseeable. [Gaines v. Monsanto Co., 655 S.W.2d 568 Mo. Ct. App. 1983]

$300,000 AWARDED TO MANUFACTURER
AGAINST PINKERTON FOR THEFTS
BY SECURITY GUARD

The security guard was involved in three thefts of gold from the plaintiff. The security firm was found liable for negligent hiring because it failed to contact character references and former employers. The court stated that when an employee is hired for a sensitive occupation, mere lack of negative evidence may not be sufficient to discharge the employer's obligation of reasonable care. [Welsh Mfg v. Pinkerton's Inc., 474 A.2D 436 (R.I. 1984)]

> How is it that a man with a criminal record that includes two arrests for possession of drugs and weapons is hired [as a guard] to protect a high school?
> That . . . officer has been arrested again—this time for allegedly firing 12 shots from a . . . handgun into the car of some youths who had been goading him. . . . Two of the youths were killed.

Many security officers are hired without having their backgrounds checked, and many have little or no training. (*Security Management*, November 1991)

MALL STORE EMPLOYEE RAPED; SUES MALL OWNER AND ANCHOR TENANT

When an employee at a mall store was raped, she sued both the mall owner and an anchor tenant who was allegedly responsible for the maintenance of the common areas under the lease. The plaintiff claimed that the defendants should have hired security guards. Because the two defendants had constructive knowledge of three previous armed robberies in the mall, they had a duty "to discover criminal acts being committed or likely to be committed on [the] property. [A] high degree of foreseeability had been established by the proof of the prior similar incidents of violent crime . . . and therefore the duty of care owed to plaintiffs includes the hiring of security guards." [California Court of Appeal, 1st District, Lisa P. v. Bingham, No. A068153]

LIABILITY AND NEGLIGENT HIRING

The common denominator of all loss prevention and security programs is people. Of what value are fences, lights, and alarm systems; guards with dogs and guns; or locks and bolts, if the people you hire lack the skills, integrity, education, and trustworthiness you require?

The three elements of negligence are duty, breach, and damages. Employers have the *duty* to exercise duly diligent inquiry into the suitability of persons they hire. Should an employer *breach* that duty by failing to make a proper inquiry of a person who subsequently injures another, thereby causing *damages*, there will be legal cause for negligent hiring. Negligent hiring is direct liability imposed for the employer's own negligence. It is the failure of an employer to exercise due (or reasonable) care in selecting an applicant in consideration of the risk created by the position to be filled.

The negligent hiring doctrine goes beyond holding an employer answerable for employees' acts in the line of duty. For example, the employer might have avoided the assault by the mail room clerk (reported above) if he had taken due care in preemployment screening. In other words, you must screen applicants adequately before you hire them.

POSITIONS OF PUBLIC TRUST REQUIRE EMPLOYEES THE PUBLIC CAN TRUST

An adequate screening, with proper adjudication of the results, may allow you to foresee and avoid legal injury. If you hire a person without checking his or her background, you may expose your firm to the risk of liability. This is especially true for certain positions of public trust, such as:

♦ Guard
♦ Child care attendant
♦ Hospital staff
♦ Private duty nurse
♦ Home health care workers
♦ Day care staff
♦ Nursing home staff
♦ Elementary and middle school faculty
♦ Playground attendant
♦ Resident manager
♦ School bus driver

In addition, you need to consider the type of access your employee will have. The person may not deal directly with vulnerable people, as would employees in the above positions, but he or she may have access to material that could make a large population vulnerable, such as:

♦ Narcotics
♦ Explosives
♦ Chemicals
♦ Ammunition

♦ Weapons
♦ Nuclear power
♦ Master keys

And then there is access to devices that could make people vulnerable, such as:

♦ Semitrailers
♦ Hotel Shuttle Vans
♦ Locomotives
♦ Aircraft
♦ Taxis

Finally, there is access to information whose compromise could incur liability or violate privacy, two types of legal harm. Check these, for example:

♦ Trade secrets
♦ Recipes
♦ Design data
♦ Marketing plans
♦ Bidding strategies
♦ Personal medical information
♦ Consumer credit reports
♦ Customer lists
♦ Results of market research

HIRE SAFE!

Make sure that your employees' emotional stability, reliability, and trustworthiness are such that entrusting them with the care or assets of other people will be clearly in the best interest of those people. You maintain control by using a personnel security program (later, I will call it a Personnel Reliability Program). For example, you don't hire a man on parole for child molestation to be a child care attendant. The ultimate decision to entrust an employee with the care or assets of others must be a reasonable, prudent decision based on review of all available facts; this is called adjudication.

Expect a return on all your investments. Employees are investments. Think about how much you invest in the process of recruiting, screening, hiring, and training. If you want the hiring process to pay off, ensure that you have sufficient information about your new hires to make sound hiring decisions. Remember that each decision to hire affects other employees, their families, and your future.

And remember that once you hire a person, he or she can influence your profit. Employees can give you a competitive edge, or they can give your competitors the edge. So there's a clear need to assure that after you hire (i.e., trust) a person, that person's emotional stability, health, reliability, and trustworthiness remain a matter for continuing assessment.

VITAL STATISTICS

[T]he biggest . . . security threat of the 1990s will continue to be employee theft—by computer, briefcase, or lunch box.

...THOMAS W. WATHEN, CEO, PINKERTON'S (*Security*, April 1991)

29% of résumés are fraudulent.

...DAVID KARAS, MARKETING MANAGER, EQUIFAX (*Security*, May 1991)

AS IF THAT WEREN'T ENOUGH

In the *Salary and Employment Trends Survey* for 1996, conducted by Career Horizons, Inc. in New York, 31% of business respondents reported increased personnel turnover during the preceding 12 months; 17% reported greater tardiness; and 15% had experienced greater absenteeism. The two leading causes of turnover were resignations, at 69%, and terminations, 37%. Employee departures are expensive. Here's why. Consider that each of those employees who was frequently late or absent, or who got fired, had spent about 45 hours a year in training, and received:

- 11 vacation days
- 9 holidays
- 8 sick days
- 3 personal days
- 5 days for miscellaneous reasons

Wait, there's more. Benefit costs for each of those turned-over employees amounted to 51.9% over direct salary costs. The benefit costs were:

- Payroll Liabilities — 12.8%
- Health/Pension Benefits — 24.0%
- Vacation/Days Off — 12.1%
- Miscellaneous Costs — 3.0%

TWO EXAMPLES OF COSTS OF BENEFITS

The computed 1995 national salary averages for Administrative Assistant and Bookkeeper were $502 and $700 per week, respectively. Benefit costs of 51.9% over those salaries are $762.54 and $1,063.30, or $39,652.08 and $55,291.60 per year. These salary expenses notwithstanding, *only 31% of employer respondents said that they routinely conduct background checks.*

Employers are spending as much as $55,000 on an employee's salary while keeping their fingers crossed that each employee is suitable, trustworthy, and nonviolent! The cost of a basic background check, to include previous employers, education, criminal record, driver record, and education, is about $67. *That's exactly 0.00121% of $55,000!*

STRATEGY FOR IMPROVEMENT

You need a strategy to:

- Reduce your exposure to liability
- Maintain your productivity

- Verify applicant skills, training, and education
- Verify applicant suitability
- Reduce your cost of turnover

That strategy consists of nine improvement options:

1. Establish a Personnel Security Program (often called a Personnel Reliability Program, or PRP).
2. Give one person the responsibility and the authority for the program.
3. Establish written security standards for all positions.
4. Consult your attorney.
5. Conduct a risk assessment.
6. Hand to each employee a written policy of security measures.
7. Verify every entry on the employment application.
8. Use skill, honesty, and personality testing where appropriate.
9. Use preemployment background checks.

A PRP consists of all measures taken to ensure the trustworthiness, reliability, and suitability of a company's human resources.

THE MENU, PLEASE

Here's some advice that will save you money and time. First, assume a worst-case scenario. Say you've just hired a man with a history of violence to work as a computer programmer in your controller's office. Second, ask yourself three questions:

1. What's the worst injury he could perpetrate against my company?
2. How much would it cost to recover?
3. How much would it cost to recruit, screen, hire, and train a replacement?

Third, consider improvement options that are tested and proven to prevent loss. For your convenience, I have provided in Figure 4.1 a menu of the components found in a quality Personnel Reliability Program.

COMPONENT	FEATURES	BENEFITS
Résumé	Subjective account of background	Quick scan for matching background with job requirements
Employment Application	Objective account of background	Comparison with résumé will reveal consistency, contradiction or outright lies. This quick evaluation will result in either a decision to continue processing for hire, or to cut losses by ending the process.
	Signed and dated, it becomes a veritable map of the person's background, provided you *require that each question be answered,* and that dates be provided for residences, employment, and education.	In-depth verification will be straightforward; possible by telephone interview; computer, and letter. Cross-checking will be facilitated, in case you require additional information.
	Affirmation of truth by virtue of signature.	This is a legal document. If you properly word it, the employment application can support you in case you must release the person for falsifying or misrepresenting information.
Initial Interview	Reveals attire, behavior, command of language, poise, and grooming	Answers basic questions: Does this person fit our firm's image? Are essential job requirements met? Do the résumé and the application match the person? What is the appicant's attitudes toward people? Toward our firm?
Follow-up Interviews	Conducted after job offer, after favorable results of background screen, psychological testing, and drug testing	Opportunity to implement ADA, Title VII, and other laws, as appropriate. Saves time and money by focusing on a person shown to be a potential asset.
Skills Testing	Objective verification of claimed skills	Save time and money by verifying before you hire OR determine extent of training required.
Integrity or Honesty Testing	Standardized test of propensity to lie, cheat, and steal; propensity to suffer others to do so without reporting it; tendency toward violence	Save time, money, and adverse publicity by revealing either portent or promise in the applicant to, and . . . Protect Your Assets!

Figure 4.1   Your Personnel Reliability Program

COMPONENT	FEATURES	BENEFITS
Pre-employment Screen, Basic	Verifies information furnished by the applicant	Verifies √Education √Employment √Driver Record

	Searches public records by county within a multiple-state region	Uncovers
		√Criminal and Civil
		  Records
		√Federal, Civil, and
		  Criminal Records

	Provides Consumer Credit Report	Reveals information regarding financial status
Pre-employment Screen, METRO-Wide	All of the above, plus . . . Searches criminal records in a metropolitan area	Searches every felony in criminal courts in the METRO area you select
Background Investigation	Searches all of the above, plus personal contact	Verifies √Bankruptcies, Liens and Judgements √DMV-Property Records √Property Ownership Search √Telephone Interviews
Adjudication	Evaluation, analysis, objective decision to hire, not hire, or to request further information	Management decision is based on objective, verified information
		Reduces legal exposure resulting from negligent hiring
		Saves time, money, resources in HR

Figure 4.1 Continued

Your business may not need all the components, but to stay alive and prosper into the millennium, you do need some assurance that your next hire won't cost you your job. *Or your life.*

You've just been introduced to the world of CI BIs, or counterintelligence background investigations. Private industry calls them preemployment checks. There's a problem with that title. A person's behavior in a position of trust must be a matter for continuing concern and periodic reviews throughout the tenure of employment. Most characteristics of potential troublemakers in your workplace can be attributed as well to potential traitors. Should these attributes not show up at initial hiring, rest assured they will surface later. The questions then become: (1) Will anyone notice? and (2) If they do notice, will they report the anomalous behavior?

Here are some clues for spotting a traitor or troublemaker. The following list of attributes comes from a U.S. Government newsletter. The attributes were gleaned from an analysis of case histories of traitors to the United States. They were then checked against histories of persons convicted of crimes of violence in the workplace. While not all attributes matched, a statistically significant number appeared to be factors in the personalities of both populations.

1. Desire for revenge: an employee may become disgruntled either because he has been terminated, or a friend has been terminated.
2. Desire for recognition after years of hard work without any thanks from the employer.
3. Abuses alcohol or other drugs.
4. Living beyond his means; burdened by nondischargeable debt.
5. Frequently seeks information for which he has no need to know.
6. A pattern of marital infidelity.
7. Serious, continuing marital problems.
8. A pattern of promiscuity.
9. Displays emotional instability.
10. Continually degrades the American form of government (not related to partisan politics, or disliking certain persons in government).
11. A pattern of entering the workplace very early, before others arrive.
12. A pattern of remaining in the workplace late, after others depart.
13. A pattern of travel to distant locations or countries, inconsistent with stated personal interests or financial means.
14. Frequent outbursts of anger; verbally abusive.

AFFECTIVE DISORDERS

A typical affective or mood disorder is characterized by periods of depression. Another affective disorder is characterized by periods of excessive elation. Frequently, the two are seen in the same person, at alternating times. Once called manic depressive illness, the proper name of this illness is now bipolar disorder. Those who suffer from bipolar disorder function quite well while on medication; they integrate fully into work, social, and academic environments. Unfortunately, the side effects from medications are often so debilitating and intrusive that a patient will stop taking the medication. Without medication, people afflicted with this disorder do remain in touch with reality ("grounded" in mental health jargon), but they may see themselves as losing control. They may then become nervous, easily agitated, compulsive, and could even tend to faint easily.

PERSONALITY DISORDERS

A person with a personality disorder is one who demonstrates inflexible and maladaptive behavior and thoughts, which persist over a long period and which interfere with his daily life or that of people close to him. Here is a list of a few of these disorders: Paranoid, Schizoid, Narcissistic, Antisocial, Borderline, Compulsive, Passive Aggressive. Victims of these illnesses manifest behaviors that are pyschopathological. Some of those behaviors include:

- ◆ Impaired reality testing, insight, and judgment
- ◆ Impaired frustration tolerance and impulse control. These persons, when angry, act out their agitation through violence

Such behaviors are usually, but not always, controllable by medication. However, there is a great risk of noncompliance with the medication schedule. Patients who discontinue their medications become unpredictable and may again become violent, exhibitionistic, and aggressively antisocial.

COLLECTION MANAGEMENT

This is what my editor would call a *non sequitur*. What does collection management have to do with mental illnesses and personnel security? Answer: *Risk and vulnerability*. People who are taking prescription medication in order to be able to accomplish their daily activities are always at risk. While medication may be prescribed for a myriad of other reasons, in the case of mental illness, the patients taking the medications are vulnerable to extortion, manipulation, and intimidation. There is always a stigma attached to mental illness, so its victims may be undergoing treatment in secret. They are vulnerable to pressure of exposure. The astute collector (another trade term for spy) will be looking for just such a vulnerability as he profiles his targets for recruitment.

Recruiting sources is what this part of the chapter is all about. You can call the sources agents, locals, or traitors. Just remember that to us, a spy is a person who, on behalf of his own country, obtains information of economic or political value about another country, while operating in that country.

A trainee for the position of foreign collection agent may spend two years studying how to recruit sources. Only in the movies does the spy do all the spying himself. In real life, he would never satisfy all of his tasks like that. Nor would he want to expose himself to the FBI. (Yes, you've read about them being caught in sting operations in the United States; I didn't say that they were all brilliant operatives.) The agent operating in a target country must have people in the right places collecting information of intelligence value for him. But one does not just go up to an engineer in a government contractor firm and ask him to start forking over classified or proprietary information. Developing reliable sources is the most sensitive aspect of HUMINT. It is also the most important, for an agent's success depends on his ability to recruit quality sources.

HOW SOURCES ARE RECRUITED

Here, for the first time in print, are the nine steps that spies use to develop sources. This method is used by foreign agents, competitor intelligence agents, law enforcement officers, private investigators, and counterintelligence agents.

1. Reconnaissance or Scouting
   Basic questions are addressed in this first step. What do we need? Where do we find it? What types of skills or positions have access to the information we want?

2. Identification

Get the names, addresses, and telephone numbers of some likely targets. Look for one or two that appear to be in the best positions. (These include, but are not limited to, secretary, janitor, file clerk, communications specialist, computer technician, and so on.) The best ones will be profiled as likely candidates or unlikely candidates, based on their access (to the information required) and their vulnerabilities (to pressure or inducements).

3. Vetting

One candidate human target at a time is vetted in the most thorough manner possible. The agent learns all there is to know about his proposed source. This vetting is similar to a complete background investigation, except that the typical BI doesn't probe into all the partners in the target's sex life (and *their* partners and spouses); the brand and type of liquor he drinks; how he combines the liquor and the sex; and the details of his mental illness, what kind of medication he takes, and how he behaves when he discontinues his medication.

4. Profile

All the information from the BI is analyzed. Further inquiry is made when necessary to establish likes and dislikes. That includes books, ice cream, sex, cars, hobbies, restaurants, foods, and more. If the agent likes the target so far, the agent may initiate a remote electronic surveillance on the man's home. Every intimate detail of his private life is recorded. The frequency and nature of sexual relations; whether he drinks before his encounters; names of friends, associations, outside activities, and clubs—all are recorded, identified, and analyzed. The most important step in this sequence is number five. Everything must be perfectly arranged for the . . .

5. Approach

This is the most sensitive part of the operation. If a male agent is approaching a woman, he takes even greater care than he would for a male source, lest he scare her off. The initial approach may be brief, perhaps momentary. Let's say the agent has established that the female target takes her lunch on a particular bench in the park each Tuesday. He strolls by, drops a piece of paper, and continues on. She calls him back. He thanks her, engages her in a two-minute conversation, and leaves. The next time he "happens" to meet her, they are in an elevator, and he can say, "Aren't you the lady from the bench near the petunias? . . . " Another favorite first meeting involves driving into the target's car in a parking lot. The agent leaves name, address, telephone number, and you can guess the rest.

6. Cultivation

   This is the second most sensitive part of the recruitment. Historically, it has taken years to cultivate a worthwhile source at high government levels. A quality cultivation will certainly take months. The agent's experience, training, and insight are severely tested in this game of perseverance and intuition. If he becomes impatient and makes a play for information too early in the relationship, the entire operation may have been for naught. He is actually building a relationship that will have to endure one of the most trying experiences in the history of humanity: betrayal. The agent is preparing to corrupt an American's loyalty, family values, morals; he's going to buy a soul. When the agent has the target's trust and respect, and perhaps even love, and the agent has catalogued all the target's human vulnerabilities for subsequent exploitation, then, and only then, is the agent ready for the next step.

7. Request

   This is the time. This is the moment. "Say, old friend, my business hasn't been so great lately. Do you suppose you could get me the organization chart for your company, so I can do a little marketing?" Nobody says no. The next time it's the production schedule for the micro-something. Maybe later on, the names of the engineers and executives working on this project. None of these documents is proprietary. Finally, after several weeks or even months: "Listen, thanks to you, I've finally clicked with my information business. Now I want to show my appreciation. There's $5,000 in it for you if you get me the spec sheet for the ROM2000." When that transaction takes place, it is videotaped, along with the source signing a receipt for the cash.

8. The Hook

See, that was so smooth, you didn't even notice what happened. The agent set the Hook. The source just sold company secrets for $5,000. And he signed a receipt for the money. And he made his first business video. In fact, the agent probably already had the names of all the engineers and scientists who work for the company. He just needed to set the Hook, in order to prepare the source for subsequent requests.

The Hook is the videotaped evidence of the source compromising himself. The videotape of the transaction and its accompanying conversation will be used for blackmail and extortion. The agent, or handler, will use it to pressure the source into giving him trade secrets. The source, from this point on, is in an emotional quicksand. He has one chance to extricate himself: he could go immediately to his security manager and reveal the entire matter. This rarely happens, because a basic need has driven the source to this point. The "Order of Need," to coin a phrase, is cash, revenge, and excitement.

After the first time, the turning point when the source actually becomes a traitor to this country or employer, the rest is easy. He comes to rely on his handler for his every need. His handler becomes his father, friend, confidant, and loan officer. If the handler or recruiter has done his job well, the source will perceive but one path from now one: cooperate with the handler and make the handler happy. It's a little like being hooked on illicit drugs. When the source considers the alternative to continued cooperation, he sees the agony of withdrawal—physical and mental anguish.

9. Pressure and Product

"By Friday, I need the source code to the corporate network encryption system. I'll pay twice what you usually get. What do you mean, you can't? I've been paying you for six months now. Would you like to see the videotapes? And copies of the receipts you signed in black ink? What do you suppose your wife would say about this? Do you need some extra money for that vacation? It's yours, right now. What do you mean, you don't feel right? You felt fine when you sold me those diskettes with the marketing and budget information on them. You felt fine when you took that little redhead on the business trip. So it's a date. The encryption system by Friday."

ADJUDICATIVE GUIDELINES FOR DETERMINING ELIGIBILITY FOR POSITIONS OF PUBLIC TRUST AND CONFIDENCE

The adjudicative process is an examination of a sufficient period of a person's life to make an informed determination that the person is trustworthy, suitable, and stable. The process is the careful weighing of a number of variables known as the whole person concept. All available, reliable information about the person should be considered in reaching a decision to hire, promote, or retain. In evaluating the relevance of a person's behavior, the adjudicator should consider the following factors:

- The nature, extent, and seriousness of the conduct
- The frequency and recency of the conduct
- The person's age and maturity at the time of the conduct
- The presence or absence of attempts at rehabilitation
- Motivation for the conduct
- The likelihood of continuation or recurrence of the conduct

Each case must be judged on its own merits. The decision to hire, retain, or promote is always the responsibility of management. Any doubt concerning persons being considered for a position of public trust should be resolved in favor of the public. The ultimate determination must be based on common sense, prevailing law (e.g., the Americans With Disabilities Act; Title VII of the Civil Rights Act of 1964; etc.), and an acceptable level of risk. Consideration must be given to the following ten criteria, called the Criteria for Adjudication:

1. Foreign Influence
2. Foreign Preference
3. Sexual Behavior
4. Inappropriate Personal Conduct

5. Irresponsible Financial History
6. Alcohol Abuse
7. Illicit Drug Use
8. Emotional, Mental, and Personality Disorders
9. Criminal Conduct
10. Misuse of Automated Information Systems

Although adverse information concerning a single criterion may not be sufficient to make an individual ineligible for hire, retention, or promotion, the person may be disqualified if there is a recent or recurring pattern of questionable judgment, irresponsibility, or emotionally unstable behavior.

However, notwithstanding the whole person concept, consideration for employment may be terminated in the face of credible derogatory information. When such information becomes known about an employment applicant or current employee, the adjudicator should consider whether the person:

♦ Voluntarily reported the information
♦ Sought assistance and followed professional guidance
♦ Resolved or appears likely to resolve the concern
♦ Should be temporarily suspended pending final adjudication of the information

If, after evaluating derogatory information regarding a current employee, the adjudicator decides that the information is not serious enough to warrant termination, it may be appropriate to recommend retention with a warning that future incidents of a similar nature may result in termination or legal action, or both. Following are commentaries on the ten criteria for adjudication.

Foreign Influence

This risk may exist when a person's family or others with whom the person has a close, continuing relationship are not citizens of the United States and may be subject to duress. This may present an unacceptable risk to companies that compete on the international market, or to those who contract to the U.S. Government. The condition could create the potential for foreign influence that might result in the compromise of a company's critical or sensitive information.

Foreign Preference

When an individual working in the United States offers allegiance to a country other than the United States, the person may be prone to provide that foreign country with critical information from your company.

Sexual Behavior

If a person's sexual behavior involves a criminal offense, indicates a personality or emotional disorder, subjects the individual to coercion or blackmail, or reflects a lack of judgment or discretion, the adjudicator should consider it disqualifying.

Inappropriate Personal Conduct

The adjudicator should consider as disqualifying any conduct that displays untrustworthiness, unreliability, or unwillingness to comply with rules or the law.

Irresponsible Financial History

Unexplained affluence may result from proceeds from profitable criminal acts. Continuous financial distress, or living outside one's means, may require a person to engage in unlawful activity to support a particular lifestyle.

Alcohol Abuse

Excessive consumption of alcohol impairs judgment, adversely effects reliability, and reduces impulse control. This behavior increases the risk that a person will harm another on your property, or disclose your sensitive business information.

Illicit Drug Use

A person may abuse drugs whose possession and sale are unlawful. The person may also abuse drugs that he or she is taking under personal prescription. In either case, the person's judgment is impaired and places your assets in jeopardy.

Emotional, Mental, and Personality Disorders

The disorders themselves impair a person's reasoning, social functioning, and occupational skills. In many cases, the medications prescribed to attenuate the symptoms may cause the patient such severe side effects that he or she discontinues the medication. Mentally ill people are not bad, but they are impaired. It is cruel and ignorant to deny employment to, for example, a person diagnosed with clinical depression or bipolar disorder. On the other hand, lithium, the drug often prescribed, can cause nausea, tremors, drowsiness, dizziness, and other symptoms that may interfere with a person's activities of daily living.

Criminal Conduct

If you want to deny employment to persons with a history of criminal convictions, put that policy in writing and enforce it all the time. Just be careful how you adjudicate certain types of records. It would be unenlightened to deny employment as a truck driver to a person convicted of trespassing. If, however, that person has three convictions for assault with a deadly weapon, you would do well to eliminate him from consideration.

Misuse of Automated Information Systems

Read the next chapter carefully to identify indicators of inappropriate behavior with technology systems.

5

How to Protect Your Automated Information: Challenge 2001

TWO APPROACHES TO INFORMATION SECURITY

Information security consultants use two approaches to AIS security: computer science and security management. (By the way, "AIS" means automated information systems. That's a lot more precise than "computer security," which really means nothing at all!) The computer science approach addresses such topics as audit trails, passwords, log-on procedures, and compartmentation.

The security management approach addresses physical security, information security, and personnel security. The competent AIS security consultant is familiar with both approaches. He or she can explain the benefits of each one.

The best way to get acquainted with your AIS security consultant is to ask questions. Here are eight questions to get you started. Compare your consultant's answers with ours.

1. What is AIS security?

   AIS security protects automated information whose loss, alteration, or denial would cost you money, embarrassment, or legal consequences. It protects the confidentiality, integrity, and availability of automated information.

2. Why do I need AIS security?

   Because people commit computer crime. For example, compromise of third-party medical data or a customer list could result in the collapse of your business.

3. Who is the typical computer criminal?

   Just about anyone at all who has either direct (keyboard) or indirect (modem) access to your computer.

4. What is computer crime?

   It could be theft, damage, or misuse of hardware, software ("floppy disks"), or documentation. Or it could be theft, misuse, or manipulation of the information in the computer, or in the raw data before it is entered into the AIS. If information is the target of the crime, you may never realize that your information has been tampered with. Or you may find out later on, when your information either disappears off the disk, turns into gibberish, or is used by your competitors.

5. Why would anyone want to do these things?

   Any number of reasons:

   ◆ Revenge
   ◆ Personal or financial gain
   ◆ Challenge
   ◆ Entertainment

6. How do these crimes happen?

   Sometimes, the only crime is that the custodian of the information failed to properly safeguard it. Any of the following could incur loss indirectly:

   ◆ Lack of contingency planning
   ◆ No security training
   ◆ Lack of audit trails

- Lack of log-on procedures
- Compromise of passwords
- Allowing terminating employees to have access to computers
- Unlimited access (no compartmentation of information)

Any of the following would incur loss directly:

- Data diddling at the keyboard (entering data different from those intended by originator)
- Trojan Horse
- Trap Door
- Virus
- On-Line interception of transmitted data (telephone lines are bugged for data transmission as well as for voice transmission)
- Surreptitious access to your AIS via modem (to name just a few).

7. What's a Virus?

A virus code is a computer program. The best analogy is a cancer virus. In its simplest form, the computer virus embeds itself in an existing program and reproduces itself. The reproductions insert themselves into other programs, both system software and applications. The infected software executes the virus program during normal processing, such as copying. That's how the virus spreads outside the original system. Another form of virus may reside on your hard disk, quiescent, for months. Suddenly, at a given date and time, it attacks. All the data and programs on your hard disk are destroyed. Or some are destroyed, while others are left seemingly in tact. But they're not intact; they're infected. What appear to be healthy programs now contain clones of the virus. They just lie there, waiting. . . .

Your risk of infection is greatest if you network. And if you have ever fired an employee who had access to your computer system, you may already be infected, because the greatest threat to your information comes from within. (Or from someone who was within, and who is now without.) Remember that we are working in an era when it is a moral obligation . . . to break into the White House computer system.

The virus could become an instrument of freedom. . . .

HACKING IS ART.

...*HARPER'S MAGAZINE* (March 1990)

8. How can I deter computer crime?

Remember that we said that there are two approaches. In computer science, one safeguard might be a security kernel. This is a master control system, transparent to the user and responsive to only one trusted party. It manages all software, including the disk operating system. The kernel monitors and reports every keystroke and is used as an embedded access control system.

The security management approach to secure AIS might include intrusion detection systems, personnel security programs, and disaster preparedness plans. This approach holds that loss prevention begins at the front door, not at the keyboard. Since AIS security is comprised of physical, personnel, and information security measures, there is a plethora of loss prevention measures designed especially for automated information systems. Consult with a Certified Information Systems Security Professional (CISSP) to learn more.

HOW YOUR INFORMATION IS VULNERABLE: THE INSIDE THREAT

Employees, not hackers or spies, have unimpeded access to your information systems. They present the most insidious threat. Any employee who can access sensitive or critical information can abuse it. Employees can manipulate financial data, payroll data, programming data, and so on.

You may ask, why would they want to? We know from recent history that people do not hire into a company with the intention to commit these behaviors; something happens later on to move them in the direction of hurtful behavior. While not all this maladaptive behavior is the fault of the employer, most immediate supervisors are not attuned to the causative factors that lead to inappropriate behavior. For example, most traitors were experiencing a financial deficit or unresolvable issues in their personal lives, and they had no one at work to reach out to.

Two-thirds of traitors betray for money. However, they all told FBI interviewers that money gave them power, control, and respect. When an employee perceives that his workplace fails to empower him, wrests control from him, or disrespects him, he either leaves or retaliates.

Employees are also using company computer systems to run their own businesses. That would be bad enough, but some of those parasitic entrepreneurs are running illicit businesses. Charles Schwab in San Francisco discovered a cocaine ring among its employees. AT&T uncovered three employees operating an illicit 900 number. General Dynamics uncovered an employee who had planted a logic bomb to erase an inventory program used to track missile parts. Another employee at a different firm planted a logic bomb that wiped out 168,000 critical financial records.

CIA REVISITED

Employees eavesdrop on e-mail; intercept and destroy messages; purloin e-mail for their own use; send obscene, racist, or threatening messages. They intercept personal information, such as addresses, telephone numbers, credit information, promotion and payroll information, and more. They may post this information as is on bulletin boards, or sell it. In any event, they have violated the *confidentiality* of your automated information.

Employees may diddle your data. That is, they enter (or "keyboard") spurious or false data. They may do this to cover up another crime, or simply to get back at your company for a real or imagined wrong. The so-called wrong in one telecommunications firm was the termination of an employee for stealing. The hacker—a friend still employed by the company—avenged his friend's termination by inserting spurious names in legitimate payroll files. Data diddling violates the *integrity* of your automated information. It may cause your company to act unlawfully, based on inaccurate information.

Employees steal information all the time. Sometimes the theft is surreptitious. You do not know information has been copied until you read about it in the newspaper, or see your product brought to market by a competitor. Sometimes, the employee will simply lock you out. You cannot retrieve the information at all, or the hacker posts a notice advising you that if you attempt to manipulate your own files, they will self-destruct. He has compromised the *availability* of your automated information.

These are the people you have probably hired without a background check. These are the people about whom you know nothing, people who remain anonymously imbedded in your automated information systems like a deadly virus in your body. These are the people you're paying to sabotage your firm. I call them "infoterrorists."

WHO ARE THESE MISCREANTS?

The National Center for Computer Crime Data (NCCCD) has found that current employees account for 26% of computer crime, while ex-employees and their accomplices account for 12%. In other words, your employment pool accounts for 38% of your compromises. Students (not further defined) account for 26%, and criminals (i.e., outside hackers not previously in your employ) account for 18% of computer crime.

According to the NCCCD, 67% of computer crime is perpetrated by men of the age of 21 to 35, while men 20 and under lay claim to about 14%, and those 36 to 40 account for about 8%. Men 41 and older account for about 8%. Hackers or infoterrorists are usually first-born males or only children, born into a middle to upper-middle class white family. They are usually loners who eschew the company of others, or who are sufficiently maladaptive to be unable to socialize. Lacking human companionship, they have a lot of time on their hands.

My own research suggests that infoterrorists are usually high academic achievers. This may follow from not socializing, but there is another factor that results from lack of human companionship. They lack the benefit of being able to confide their problems to friends. Thus, they see the computer as a safe, attractive, anonymous escape from their problems. Hackers invent their own code of ethics as they go. They do not believe in the right to own information as property, but rather that all information belongs to all people. It is, therefore, acceptable to destroy others by revealing personal information on a public bulletin board.

When a hacker breaks into your system, he achieves an electronic high. He has proved that the system can be compromised, and he feels that that, above all, is his ordained destiny. He feels that the people who manage computer systems have an obligation to keep them secure. He has an obligation to reveal that the systems are not secure. He also has an obligation, even an emotional mandate, to attain control and to be in control.

A sure way for the hacker to attain control is to compromise your information. I see his self-esteem as pathologically low, thus, his perceived need for control is unending. For the social deviate we call a hacker, making someone powerless is the epitome of control. And you and your firm are powerless from the moment this culprit gets into your system. See Figure 5.1 for the profile of a hacker.

I have talked with numerous authorities in the field of hacking, including FBI special agents, about the gender of the typical hacker. It seems that there are more male than female hackers. One authority in private industry told me that in eleven years of interviewing, chasing, and prosecuting hackers, he came across only one female hacker.

INFOTERRORISM, HERE AND NOW

As I completed this chapter, President Clinton was preparing to announce the Cyber Security Assurance Group. This is to be an emergency response task force designed to manage terrorist incidents in cyberspace.

USA Today (Wednesday, June 5, 1996) carried cover and feature stories about the clear and present danger to the U.S. infrastructure by what I call infoterrorists. War strategists agree that the way to bring a country to its knees is by seizing control of its communications and broadcast systems. Consider the implications of infoterrorist compromise

Profile of a Hacker

When the hacker perceives an automated information system as poorly protected, he sees a challenge. Hacking is art. He [perceives himself as having] an obligation to break into any system that can be broken into. (Barlow et. al., March 1990)

Don't wait for a psychologist to explain why these people behave as they do. Just be aware that they are:

- Lacking in moral values
- Well educated
- Male
- Between 15 and 37
- Lacking in self esteem
- Passively resistant to authority
- Disdainful of law
- Disdainful of the rights of others
- Disdainful of loyalty
- Devious
- Narrow minded, finely focused
- Introverted
- Highly intelligent
- Patient
- Social deviates, in that they seem incapable of empathy, genuineness, warmth, defined personal goals, and respect for societal norms.

They are usually authorized users. And they represent a clear and present threat to your firm.

Barlow, J. P., Jacobson, R., Brand, R., Stoll, C., Hughes, D., Drake, F., Goldstein, E., et al. (1990, March). Forum: Is Computer Hacking a Crime? *Harper's Magazine*, pp. 46 - 57.

Figure 5.1 Profile of a Hacker

How to Protect Your Automated Information: Challenge 2001

- DO have a Risk Analysis conducted.

- DO protect unattended terminals; insist on log-outs.

- DO protect your media; lock up all removable media.

- DO back up data; back up on a daily basis, at least.

- DO use an audit and access control system for your AIS.

- DO use physical, information, and personnel security to control access to automated information systems.

- DO protect your passwords.

- DO test new software for viruses.

- DO remember that AIS security begins at the perimeter of your building, not at the keyboard!

- DO initiate and PRACTICE a disaster recovery plan.

- DON'T share passwords.

- DON'T leave the computer running unattended, on a LAN.

- DON'T allow unescorted visitors into any area where data is keyed or displayed.

- DON'T send computers out for repair with data files on their hard disks.

- DON'T assume that your information is protected because it's out of sight.

- DON'T allow employees to work at the keyboard during non-business hours without accounting for what they're doing.

- DON'T allow keyboard access to new hires until a background check is completed.

Figure 5.2   How to Protect Your Automated Information: Challenge 2001

Principles of Information Security

1. Information must have a dollar value assigned to it.

2. Information with a high dollar value is an asset and must be protected as such.

3. You have the right and the obligation to protect your valuable information.

4. Information is protected by controlling access to it; this requires physical as well as logical controls.

5. Automated information must be protected by an undefeatable means of recording all attempts at access.

6. Automated information systems (AIS) must be resistant to attack.

7. All magnetic media must be kept under control, whether it is in storage or in use.

8. There must be a continuing AIS Security Education Program—mandatory for all employees.

9. Each user of the AIS must have access only to that information to which he or she is specifically entitled, and no more.

10. An AIS connected to a communications link is infinitely more vulnerable to compromise than one not connected to such a link.

11. An AIS connected to a communications link must be protected at the link as well as inside the system.

12. Each person accessing your information must be held accountable for his or her behavior.

Figure 5.3   Principles of Information Security

of public switch networks, transportation nodes, finance and banking (e.g., electronic funds transfer networks), utilities and power, and military and civil government.

Consider this scenario. Air traffic control is in the hands of infoterrorists. Rail traffic switching and road traffic semaphore signals are controlled by infoterrorists. Telephone relay systems are controlled by infoterrorists. Radio and television services are being jammed. Think about it. Now what do we do? Remember that all news regarding the emergency is now being controlled by those who caused it.

HOW TO PROTECT YOUR ASSETS

Be aware. Sponsor periodic awareness programs in your firm. Teach your staff that secure information systems mean secure jobs. Aim for a no-conflict environment. Remind each person who accesses your automated information systems that the information contained therein belongs to their employer, as does the system itself. Consult with your attorney about writing a zero tolerance policy condemning any behavior that violates the confidentiality, integrity, or availability of your information. Check the backgrounds of people before you allow them access to your computers. See Figure 5.2 for a detailed list of how to protect your automated information.

You have the right and the obligation to protect your assets. It is just and prudent for you to inquire into the backgrounds of people who work in your information systems. Your corporate behavior must announce in a clear, uncompromising manner, "We will protect our information." Figure 5.3 describes the principles of information security.

6

Principles and Premises: Advice from the Professionals

On the following pages, you will find succinct guidance for protecting your assets. Most loss prevention practitioners follow these principles and premises. You will find that they apply common sense to a broad range of loss prevention issues. They should also provoke you to reflect about the level of quality that you want your loss prevention program to attain. The information is provided to help you make informed choices about your counterespionage, OPSEC, and security programs.

PRINCIPLES OF LOSS PREVENTION MANAGEMENT

1. Loss Prevention is a body of knowledge whose application to a given environment attenuates loss from natural disasters, accidents, or malice.
2. All professionally designed Loss Prevention programs are based upon the probability of occurrence of loss-inducing events. From this principle evolve two key issues in crime liability: *foreseeability* and *due care.*

3. Loss Prevention is a function of management; a successful LP program is one which is fully supported by management. The protection of assets is a means to retain profit and increase production; the successful asset protection program is managed like a successful business. Every successful business has interconnecting networks of control. To protect your assets, you must be in control.

PREMISES FOR LOSS PREVENTION

We must assert some premises as a foundation for a loss prevention program, namely:

1. Of all the loss-inducing agents, people cause the greatest losses.
2. We cannot determine by looking at or talking with a person whether he or she will cause a loss. It is, therefore, reasonable and prudent to find an acceptable level of risk in order to attenuate a portion of inevitable loss. The acceptable level of risk is the potential loss or liability that you are willing to assume without instituting security measures or purchasing insurance. The best example of an acceptable level of risk is a deductible: you underwrite that amount yourself and are willing to pay it out of pocket.
3. Each person, family, and business has the right and the obligation to protect against loss. The exercise of that right is prudent behavior, not an affront to anyone's integrity.

PRINCIPLES OF SECURITY MANAGEMENT

1. Security is a system of interrelated barriers. In physical security, barriers are lights, fences, dogs, locks, intrusion detection systems, vehicle barriers, terrain contours, plants, and human response. These barriers are placed in a system that is designed to provide delay time and exposure.

   In personnel security, barriers are those physical activities and reasoning processes used in determining the integrity, loyalty, and trustworthiness of employees and employment candidates.
2. Security education and awareness are part of security management.

3. All professionally designed security programs are based on the analyses of Assets, Threat, Vulnerability, and Impact. Impact analyses identify the benefits and costs of maintaining each asset at various levels of protection.
4. In a secured environment, each person is accountable for her own behavior; all activities are capable of being audited.
5. Cost-effective security evolves from consistent interaction with other disciplines of management science; these include, but are not limited to, decision sciences, personnel management, marketing, and risk management. In addition, architects and engineers must play a key role in the conceptualization, design, and application of access control, intrusion detection systems, and closed circuit television.

PRINCIPLES OF PERSONNEL SECURITY: THE PERSONNEL RELIABILITY PROGRAM

1. A person's emotional stability, reliability, and trustworthiness must be such that trusting her with the care of other people or their valued assets will be clearly in their best interest.
2. The ultimate decision to entrust a person with the care of others or their assets must be a reasonable, prudent decision based on review of all available facts.
3. There is a clear need to assure that after the initial determination is made to hire (i.e., trust) a person, the person's emotional stability, health, reliability, and trustworthiness remain a matter for continuing assessment.
4. The initial decision to entrust a person with responsibility, and the decision to continue to trust a person, are exclusively the responsibility of management.
5. Management adherence to Principles 1, 2, and 3 increases the ability to exercise due care, foresee loss, and probably avoid it.

ESSENTIALS OF PHYSICAL SECURITY

While this manual is about information and personnel security, you should know that physical security is the third of the three basic security disciplines. Note how the following principles are similar to and complement the other two disciplines.

1. The epitome of physical security is interrelated barriers.
2. The framework for interrelated barriers is defensible space.
3. The first consideration in the design of a security system is response.
4. The more time you invest in planning response, the less time you will spend defending lawsuits.
5. A balanced security system will protect against the defined threat and provide an appropriate response. This is called the Rule of Parsimony. Buy and apply only what you need. Protecting against undefined threat is an unnecessary expense.
6. Architects and engineers play an integral role in the design of a balanced security system.
7. No security measures must ever be undertaken without an analysis of assets, threat, vulnerability, and impact.
8. The Crime Formula, as you will read in the next chapter, is an essential component of threat analysis.
9. There is no such thing as a free physical security survey. Reputable professionals do not work without compensation.

7

Three Formulas for Success

THE CRIME FORMULA

$$Crime = \frac{Inclination + Opportunity}{Resistance}$$

A professionally designed security system reduces opportunity and increases resistance. When you examine this formula, it is easy to see why U.S. business loses billions each year to employee theft, workplace violence, and industrial espionage. People steal, kill, and commit espionage in the workplace because they have the inclination to do so, because the workplace provides ample opportunity, and because employers offer little resistance. They take few precautions to prevent, detect, or deter crime.

One woman, the CEO of a high-tech firm, made an observation that epitomizes what the crime formula is about. She said:

> We had a commercial artist design a tasteful sign which we posted in a conspicuous place in our personnel office. It says,
>> Be careful what you put in your employment application. We'll check every word.
>> Be careful what drugs you take. We'll check every drop.
> It became a game [she said] to watch how many [would-be applicants] walked out without the paperwork after reading that sign.

Now there's someone who knows how to protect her assets. That sign is an up-front, no-nonsense deterrent. So are the background screening and drug tests the sign warns about. Most employers are not afraid to use these tools of resistance, once they know about them. But there is one thing some employers seem to fear. That is doing their civic duty. Here's an example.

A male assaults a woman while both are employed by Employer A. The man is arrested, charged, and released on bail. The employer terminates him for having committed felonious assault on the premises. That former employee, while awaiting trial, applies for a position elsewhere. When the prospective employer checks references, Employer A fails to inform the reference checker of the facts surrounding the departure of the assaultive former employee. In fact, courts have held that there must be a reasonable balance between the fear of this former employer of tortious exposure, and his *duty* to inform other members of society *in an objective, factual manner*, of the assaultive inclinations of his former employee. Private citizens have prevailed in court action against former employers who, knowing the violent tendencies of terminated employees, have failed to inform others, and in so doing, directly caused injury to victims in the hiring company. Timely, accurate, objective information is the foundation of resistance to crime.

THE PRODUCTIVITY FORMULA

$$\text{Productivity} = \frac{\text{Attitude} + \text{Skills}}{\text{Conflict}}$$

This is the management version of the Crime Formula. You may be surprised to learn that you can determine an applicant's attitudes—his attitudes toward stealing, use of illicit drugs, falsifying time cards, and much more. You can do this by administering psychological tests. (No, not the MMPI. The Minnesota Multiphasic Personality Inventory isn't an appropriate preemployment test. It's a clinical test to help determine the nature and extent of mental illness. There are other tests that are appropriate for preemployment screening.)

Using the proper psychological tests, you can determine with a great degree of accuracy whether an employment applicant is suited for a given position. You can determine, for example, whether a person possesses the customer relations skills necessary for a sales position.

Through inexpensive testing and background screening, and with careful interviewing, you can measure the attitude and skills of any applicant, for any position. You can also reduce the conflict that would result from drugs, or violence, or theft in the workplace.

THE PROBABILITY FORMULA

$$P = \frac{f}{n}$$

The prevention of loss is based on the probability of occurrence of discrete loss-inducing events.

The probability of the loss of a given asset can be measured. The formula, right out of a college statistics text, says that the probability of occurrence of an event (P) is the number of favorable cases (f) divided by the total number of equally possible cases (n). A favorable case is an event identical in nature to the event under consideration, such as a coin coming up heads.

The definition of frequency says that in a series of trials (such as coin tosses), the probability of an incident (P—such as the tossed coin showing heads) occurring is the ratio of the number of occurrences (f—tosses) to the total number of events (n).

Let's say, in an oversimplified but practical application, that there is a universe or population of 100 companies like yours. In that population, workplace violence occurred ten times last year. Of those ten occurrences, one person was killed in each of five different occurrences. Therefore,

$$\text{Probability of death from workplace violence} = \frac{10 \text{ incidents}}{5 \text{ deaths}}$$

or one out of two, or 50%.

Now, what's the probability that this will happen in your workplace? You guessed it:

$$P = \frac{100 \text{ companies}}{10 \text{ incidents}}$$

You have a 10% probability of experiencing workplace violence, with a 50% chance of death.

The point is, you protect your assets based on the calculations of probability, not based on somebody's sales hustle, or on a hunch about the *possibility* of something happening.

Appendix A
Whither IE in Our Day?

Biotech Spy Case Opens in Boston
Testimony resumes today in Boston in what is believed to be one of the
first criminal trials involving industrial espionage and the biotechnology
industry. Federal prosecutors say the case involves two men who
conspired to sell stolen biotechnology to the Russian KGB spy agency,
but who were tripped up by a Russian-speaking FBI agent. . . . The FBI
agent, Dimitry Droujinsky, testified Wednesday that Subu Kota of
Westboro had promised to sell him a genetically engineered growth
hormone as well as radar-deflecting paint used on Stealth bombers.
...UPI WIRE SERVICE, Boston, September 4, 1997

IS IT COMPETITOR INTELLIGENCE, OR IS IT INDUSTRIAL ESPIONAGE?

Competitor intelligence or CI is legal; industrial espionage or IE is not. CI
gleans corporate information from open sources, such as newspapers,
company brochures, and public libraries. IE steals corporate information
not intended for release to the public.

Economic Espionage Rising, FBI Director Tells Congress
Economic spying on U.S. companies by foreign governments—friend
and foe alike—is on the rise and costing the United States billions of

dollars and millions of jobs, FBI Director Louis Freeh told Congress yesterday.

...FRANK SWOBODA, *The Washington Post*, February 29, 1996

In the same article, Freeh is quoted as having articulated a list of corporate espionage victims from Mobil and IBM to McDonnell-Douglas and Schering-Plough. Swoboda further reported that the FBI Director had told a joint hearing of the Senate Judiciary and Intelligence committees that in the post-Cold War era, foreign countries are increasingly focusing their espionage efforts on U.S. economic secrets.

Later in the article, Swoboda says that Senator Arlen Specter (R-Pa.) quoted the White House Office of Science and Technology as estimating losses to U.S. businesses from foreign espionage at close to $100 billion a year. Specter estimated that at least fifty-one countries now have spies in the United States trying to steal economic secrets.

I think you will agree that these are indications of serious problems in protecting U.S. business secrets. Losing a billion dollars a year to fifty-one foreign countries is a warning that American business must tend to its own protection right now.

This Appendix is about Indications and Warnings. First, we'll take another look at the indications of foreign industrial espionage threat to American business from the 1980s to the present. Then I'll give you an updated version of target companies and target information. Next, I'll reveal more about technical tradecraft, or how spies spy. Take these last two efforts as warnings about potentially disastrous consequences for American business unless it pays close attention to preventing loss of its life blood: critical business information.

This Appendix is also about Forecasting. At the end of the Appendix, I'll offer you my opinion of where IE is going for the next three to five years—to 2003.

Nabisco, Keebler, and Frito-Lay agreed to pay $125 million to Proctor and Gamble after a 5-year battle. . . . P & G (for Duncan Hines) was planning to tell a U.S. District Court that its competitors stole a secret process for crispy . . . chewy cookies.

...*U.S. News & World Report*, September 25, 1989

THE MASTER SPIES AND THEIR AGENTS—
RUSSIA

When the U.S.S.R. collapsed in 1990, the KGB, or Soviet Committee for State Security, had been handling both internal security and the collection of foreign intelligence of strategic, technical, and scientific value for nearly seventy years, albeit under different names. It has always had directorates that specialized in different matters of espionage and state security. These included a directorate for fabricating special cover stories; one for forgeries and papers; one for internal security; one for special operations (which usually means assassinations of inept agents who have compromised an entire operation); one for processing special intelligence collection requirements from other branches of government (what were then the Soviet ministries); and many more.

Today, in December 1997, the KGB is handling internal security and collecting foreign intelligence, albeit under a different name. In December 1990, it evolved into the Ministry of Security and Internal Affairs. In late 1991, the KGB became the Federal Service for Foreign Intelligence (the abbreviation for the Russian words is SVR). Its directorates still exist and still handle intelligence collection tasks from the Ministry of Science and Technology (which is now Russian instead of Soviet). The KGB, or SVR, collects foreign intelligence of scientific and technical value. (In the United States, the term KGB is used more commonly than SVR, as you may have noticed.)

The GRU, previously the Soviet Military Intelligence Staff, became the Russian Military Intelligence Staff. But the last time I checked (in early 1997), it was the Main Intelligence Directorate of the Russian General Staff (the equivalent of our Defense Intelligence Agency, or DIA). It is tasked by the Russian Ministry of Defense to collect foreign intelligence of military value.

The Agents

John Anthony Walker and his son Michael Lance Walker were indicted on May 28, 1985 on six counts of espionage. The elder Walker, John, a retired Navy warrant officer, was charged with having sold classified material to Soviet agents for the preceding eighteen years. A Soviet embassy official, Alexei Tkachenko, on routine permanent station at the Soviet embassy in Washington, D.C., returned to Moscow within days after John Walker was arrested. On November 6, 1986, John Walker was sentenced to life imprisonment and Michael, a Navy chief petty officer, to twenty-five years. They had sold top secret cryptographic information and code cards to the KGB for over $1 million.

In January 1977, Christopher J. Boyce, an employee of TRW, Inc., a California-based Defense contractor, and his friend Andrew Daulton Lee were arrested for selling classified information to the Soviets. The pair had netted around $70,000 by passing top secret code material to the KGB in Mexico City. Lee was sentenced to life imprisonment, Boyce to forty years. In 1980, Boyce escaped and spent nineteen months as a fugitive. After authorities caught him again, they added twenty-eight years to his sentence. Robert Lindsey wrote a book called *The Falcon and the Snowman* (Simon and Schuster, 1979) based on the story of Boyce and Lee.

On Thursday, February 8, 1996, *The Daily Telegraph* carried an article written by Alan Philps in Moscow with the headline, "Yeltsin backs industrial espionage." Philps reported that Yeltsin criticized his intelligence services for making poor use of the results of industrial espionage and told them they should do more to close the technology gap with the West.

CHINA

The collection of economic and technological intelligence in the United States is priority one for China. China is not oblivious to the relationships that the United States has with Russia and her former satellite nations. Those relationships have agreements whereby we share intellectual as well as material technological knowledge. China perceives itself today in a position where it must keep up technologically merely to survive.

Further, in order to survive as a world power into the twenty-first century, China must compete with the economics that are being molded today by the joint ventures between the United States and Russia, Vietnam, and other Southeast Asian countries. China's economic espionage, then, is driven by a perceived need for national survival. Their collection platforms are efficient and cost-effective.

China's primary means of collecting economic and technological intelligence is through Chinese communities overseas. This has been true of all Asian nations for decades, and for China probably for centuries. These communities consist of Chinese businessmen, students, professionals, and scientists. Few of the collectors are in this country as permanent residents. Most are here for training, education, internships, and so on. The dichotomy between the paucity of permanent resident collectors and the plethora of temporaries is easy to explain. It is easier for Chinese foreign intelligence services to levy collection requirements on people who have family back home, and it is easier to debrief them when they return to the homeland. There has been one notable exception.

A True Professional

Larry Wu-Tai Chin had already retired from the CIA when he was arrested on November 22, 1985 and charged with committing espionage against the United States for thirty-three years on behalf of the Peoples Republic of China. He had retired from the CIA in 1981 at age 63. He was indicted on seventeen counts of espionage. On February 8, 1986, he was convicted on all counts and remanded to the Federal lockup in Alexandria, Virginia. On February 21, the retired CIA intelligence officer committed suicide in his jail cell. In 1990, intelligence analysts were still trying to figure out the extent of damage caused by Chin, to my knowledge the only foreign mole ever brought before the public eye in the United States. Chin was a professional spy for a foreign government. The Americans identified in this book as having engaged in espionage were traitors.

JAPAN

Japan has three excellent in-place platforms for collecting industrial and economic information abroad: (1) trade organizations permanently located within a target country; (2) Japanese companies, or those co-owned by Japanese, located in the target country; and (3) Japanese communities overseas. In addition, Japanese executives and technical personnel in Japan frequently arrange visits to U.S. companies in this country. The visitors frequently combine competitor intelligence with industrial espionage. American business encourages these visits, welcoming Japanese businessmen with open arms.

I have found no information that would lead me to believe that U.S. businessmen visiting Japanese industries in Japan are welcomed with the same *mi casa es su casa* embrace. The Japanese are intelligent, insightful, and industrious. They are not afflicted with the naiveté requisite to giving away their secrets, as American business has been.

After reading the foregoing, you can understand why Japan has hitherto seen no need for a formal intelligence apparatus. However, as mentioned earlier in this book, they are adroit intelligence collectors.

The Collectors

Ronald Hoffman was a senior rocket scientist for Science Applications International Corporation in California, where he was managing a secret Air Force contract. During the period from 1986 to 1990, he sold to Japanese firms some of those secrets, worth hundreds of millions of dollars in U.S. research efforts. Two of the firms—Mitsubishi and Nissan—paid him some $750,000. He was caught in a sting operation and drew six years in prison.

FRANCE, ISRAEL ALLEGED TO SPY ON U.S. FIRMS

> France and Israel are denying charges by the Central Intelligence
> Agency that they engage in economic espionage against the United
> States, but documents in a report issued by the Senate Intelligence
> Committee appear to provide case studies of the two allies' spying on
> U.S. military contractors and high-tech firms.
>
> ...PAUL BLUSTEIN, *The Washington Post,* Friday, August 16, 1996

France

From 1987 to 1989, French intelligence agents (government agents, not industry representatives) gained frequent surreptitious access to the

Paris offices of IBM and Texas Instruments. The CIA learned about it, called in the FBI, and the penetrations were stopped. It seems that the French government had ordered the collection of certain types of microchips to pass to a French company called Bull. Naturally, the Department of State lodged a protest. Apparently, neither the Department of State nor France took the protest seriously, because a year or so later, Honeywell Federal Systems sold out to Bull. Bull-Honeywell, I understand, is now a major supplier to the CIA.

Israel

Jonathan Pollard, an intelligence analyst with the Naval Investigative service, and his wife were arrested by the FBI on November 21, 1985, outside the Israeli Embassy in Washington, D.C. as they were seeking asylum with the intent to flee the United States. Both were charged with selling classified documents (top secret, it turned out) to Israeli intelligence agents of the Mossad for $50,000. Later, his wife was accused of (and pleaded guilty to) intent to sell to the Peoples Republic of China U.S. analyses of China's intelligence operations in this country. On March 4, 1987, Jonathan Pollard was sentenced to life imprisonment; his wife received a five-year term. His motivation, he said, was ideological. After his imprisonment, Federal investigators concluded that he had received much more money than originally believed, that certain assertions (accusations, if you will) set forth in the legal charging papers had probably been erroneous, and that damage assessment for the compromised information would take years. They should have interviewed Victor Ostrovsky.

Ostrovsky wrote a book with Claire Hoy called *By Way of Deception: The Making and Unmaking of a Mossad Officer* (St. Martin's Press, 1990). In his book, Ostrovsky claims to have been a Mossad officer. To my knowledge, that claim has never been discredited, so let me share some of his first-hand information with you. He observes that there was an outcry in the U.S. Government about the Mossad operating in the United States when, in fact, they were not. They are, he writes, prohibited from doing so, and they respect that order. But Pollard was not recruited and handled by the Mossad. Rather, says Ostrovsky, he had been receiving $2,500 a month since early 1984 from an organization called Lishka le Kishrei Mada, or LAKAM, the Hebrew acronym for the

Israeli defense ministry's Scientific Affairs Liaison Bureau, and was spiriting secret U.S. documents to the home of Irit Erb, a secretary at the Israeli embassy in Washington, D.C. LAKAM was then headed by Rafael Eitan, who was a former Mossad agent who had taken part in the 1960 abduction of Adolf Eichmann from Argentina.

Wait, there's more. Ostrovsky says that the CIA seemed to be convinced that the Mossad, except for liaison, simply does not operate actively in the United States. But as Ostrovsky writes:

> Well, they're wrong.
>
> Pollard was not Mossad, but many others actively spying, recruiting, organizing, and carrying out covert activities—mainly in New York and Washington . . . do belong to a special, super-secret division of the Mossad called simply Al, Hebrew for "above" or "on top."
>
> The unit is so secretive, and so separate from the main organization, that the majority of Mossad employees don't even know what it does. . . . But it exists, and employs between 24 and 27 veteran field personnel, three as active katsas [agents]. *Most, though not all, of their activity is within U.S. borders* [emphasis added].

IS YOUR FIRM A TARGET?

Not all firms are eligible for espionage targeting. Quality espionage operations are managed like a quality business. They are well-planned, well-organized, well-staffed, well-directed, and well-controlled. This costs money, so collection (i.e., spying) efforts must show a Return on Investment.

In Chapter 2, you read five clues to help you decide if your company is a target. Here are five more. If you answer "Yes" to any of the following five questions, your firm is a candidate for either foreign industrial espionage, or competitor intelligence, or both.

1. Has your firm successfully competed for Defense contracts?
2. Does your firm have a history of developing breakthrough technology?
3. Does your firm compete for overseas markets?
4. Does it have contracts in support of any Middle East country?

The foregoing is not an all-inclusive list. So, if you answered "No" to all those questions, don't assume your firm is immune to espionage. Ask yourself the fifth question: Does your firm have information anyone else could use for a profit? To find the answer, let's do a quick review.

Let's focus first on some key high-technology industry targets, and then on key technology targets for espionage. In the list below, you see the prime targets in high-tech industry for foreign intelligence collection. Just remember that many foreign agents are from "friendly" countries. And some of today's friends were yesterday's enemies.

Key High-Tech Targets
Aviation Navigation Systems

Radiation Hardening for Radio Frequency Equipment

Food Preservation Techniques

Ultra-Low-Frequency Telecommunications

Space-Based Reconnaissance Systems

Waste Disposal Methods and Technology

High-Energy Laser Technology and Applications

Synthetic Motor Oil and Lubricant Technology for Tanks in Subtropical Climates

The list above shows you a few of the specific technology targets, or the targets for today's spy. Notice the broad range of topics on this list of knowledge requirements. When a tasking is composed for a specific topic, it may be called a Special Intelligence Collection Requirement.

Sometimes the line is blurred between industrial espionage and competitor intelligence (CI). CI is basic research, conducted (mostly) in public documents. Every espionage agent, investigator, academic, and researcher begins her quest for information by first conducting a literature search in the public domain.

But speaking of competitor intelligence, which of your secrets can win contracts for other companies? Many executives think they do not have information anyone else can use. Take a look at the list below. Every firm has break-evens, customer lists, margins—and health.

Yes, health. What if the Chief Executive Officer of General Motors suddenly became seriously ill? Would that have an effect on the auto industry? On the stock market? On the steel industry? How about the petroleum industry? On the other hand, what if Toyota made overtures toward him?

Now, what if one of your key executives began personal negotiations with a competitor? Suppose that key person has direct, unlimited access to certain critical business information, like marketing plans, or trade secrets? A more direct way of putting it:

What if someone stole your . . .

BIDDING STRATEGIES

BOND AND STOCK ISSUE
   PLANS

BREAKEVENS

CUSTOMER LISTS

FORMULAS

MARGINS

MERGER/ACQUISITION
   PLANS

NEGOTIATING STRATEGIES

OVERSEAS MARKETING
   PLANS

PERSONNEL HEALTH
   REPORTS

REAL ESTATE
   DEVELOPMENT PLANS

RECRUITING/SEPARATING
   STRATEGY

The compromise of any of these types of critical business information could result in legal exposure, cash loss from loss of sales, embarrassment, ruined public relations, cash loss from lost opportunity, and more.

Before I give you some details about the mechanics of spying, let me show you another list. In this list, the IE targets are unrelated to technology, but are nonetheless very valuable. Some of these topics may bring a smile; some may cause you doubt. I assure you, they are valid sources of six-figure cash bounties for skilled agents. The list is only an excerpt; the actual list runs to about four pages. I have had clients who spent megabucks to protect some of these information targets.

Non-High-Tech Targets of Industrial Espionage

ADHESIVES formulas, packaging, marketing

AUTOMOBILE design, release dates

COSMETICS formulas, packaging, and plans for shelf space at point of sale

CEREAL packaging and market introduction dates

COMMERCIAL REAL ESTATE acquisition and development plans

COOKIE recipes

DIAPER design, packaging, advertising plans

FUR and SKINS inventory, marketing plans

LINGERIE design, marketing plans (A model in Manhattan talked too much about when her line was due to retailers. She was given some money and put onto an airplane to Luxembourg. She was told to shut up and to stay put until they called her. Or else. They wanted her out of the way until the line she had been modeling was placed in stores.)

MARKET NICHE strategy

PRODUCT POSITIONING strategy

RACE HORSE BREEDING plans

RECRUITING requirements

RETOOLING plans, requirements

TOY design, packaging, market segment, market introduction dates (One marketing vice-president, suspected of selling design data to a freelance spy had his life threatened.)

These have been the most valuable secrets of the 1990s and will hold their value into the twenty-first century. No country kills for state secrets anymore. But now and then, someone gets hurt or threatened during the course of collecting quality information about these topics. They are the money-makers for spies.

PROFILE OF A SPY

The ideal spy (in my opinion) is well-educated, reads widely, and has fluent knowledge of at least three languages. This fluency allows him to understand and tolerate various cultures, beliefs, and customs. He easily internalizes the beliefs and values of his target culture or company (yours, perhaps) in order to think the way they think. He is gifted with an insatiable curiosity, is forever looking for trends and relationships, as well as for pieces that do not fit. He is resourceful, patient, tenacious, dispassionate, single-minded, and, above all, self-disciplined. He has mastered numerous skills and acquired vast knowledge, but presents himself as a person of common breeding. He is a consummate actor, an artist: he spies for the sake of spying.

He understands himself; he knows who he is; he has a mature ego. He disdains violence, treats everyone with respect, and commands respect by his demeanor and language. He may be a mercenary, offering to the highest bidder, or he may be dedicated, but not both. In other words, he is loyal to his own values.

In my experience, all professional government spies that I have known have been male. I suspect that this is true as well of industrial espionage agents.

TRADECRAFT: MORE ON HOW SPIES SPY

The threat presented by the human intelligence agent (HUMINT) is enormous. A series of successful espionage efforts against your company could bring it to bankruptcy. Having said that, I now tell you that most intelligence—political, military, economic, and industrial—is gathered by overt means, without subterfuge.

Here are some of the overt sources that agents use to obtain information about your company and its executives.

1. Public databases
2. Public documents (Moody's, Dun and Bradstreet, etc.)
3. Your newsletters
4. Your PR brochures

5. Your booth at trade shows
6. Job interviews with your company
7. Your press releases
8. Your employees (secretarial, sales, purchasing, marketing, engineering, comptroller)
   ♦ By dating them to elicit information
   ♦ By frequenting the places they frequent at lunch or after work to listen to them talk
9. The competitor intelligence firm you have retained
10. Hiring your employees

Notice that none of these methods involves any intrigue or coercion. There is nothing illegal or even unethical in any of them. The results of this phase of intelligence gathering would help an agent profile your firm's social atmosphere and single out a few individuals for special collection efforts. Let me remind you that industrial espionage methods and competitor intelligence methods are frequently indistinguishable.

Sensitivity Pays

You need to be sensitive to your firm's vulnerabilities. Your CEO, corporate security director, public relations people, and general counsel need to agree on a policy for controlling the flow of information out of your firm. Be aware—and make your employees aware—that no single source of information will compromise your operation. But many little pieces of information put together by skilled analysts over time will provide the mosaic necessary for a competitor to steal your trade secrets.

SOMEONE HAS TO OWN IT

Let me quote a passage written by James A. Schweitzer in his book *Protecting Business Information: A Manager's Guide* (Butterworth-Heinemann, 1996):

> Someone has to accept responsibility for information ownership. These data owners have the best overview or insight into appropriate information classification decisions. They best know about the value

or sensitivity of any given element of information within their area of responsibility. Value or sensitivity is the basis for assigning information classifications, and classification is the basis for determination of appropriate investment in information protection measures.

Schweitzer is telling us that we're not going to be able to protect our information unless some one person decides that it has sufficient value to warrant continuing special attention.

GETTING THE SIGNALS

Surreptitious compromise is the theft, modification, or denial of information without awareness by the owner of the information. Surreptitious compromise is nirvana for the spy and his employer. For example, how damaging would it be to your firm if your market niche strategy were acquired by a competitor without your firm knowing it? Surreptitious compromise may be accomplished by intercepting radio frequency (rf) signals, also called technical surveillance.

Here's a real life situation to give you a frame of reference for the ensuing discussion.

A high-tech firm hired a marketing director with credentials that looked impressive on his résumé. The firm did not verify those credentials. A few days before this man was hired, and by sheer coincidence, the corporate security director had asked us to demonstrate various clandestine listening devices. With the permission of the president and the assistance of the security director, we bugged a vacant suite. The suite we used had been reserved for the Director of Marketing. . . .

We placed one bug under the lip of the desk, closest to where a client would sit. Another under a coffee table on the far side of the room. Then we modified the telephone to make it a transmitter both on- and off-hook.

The company president traveled to Europe, and the corporate security director became too busy to work on the project with us. So we left the bugs in place, along with a tape player, which we had placed in the office of the corporate security director. A few weeks later, we received a phone call from an anxious and horrified president. You guessed it. When he and the security director remembered our little project, they played back the tape. It seems their newly hired Director of Marketing was working with a hidden agenda. He was boldly passing timely, accurate information to a competitor from his suite in my client's premises!

COUNTERMEASURES

There is no way you can tell if your premises have been compromised by surreptitious audio surveillance ("bugging") unless you retain a countermeasures expert. Industrial espionage agents work for extremely high stakes, as do the FBI and the SVR (formerly the KGB). Hence, they are extremely careful. They are all highly skilled and use state-of-the-art equipment. If you think you're bugged, call the experts—from a pay phone.

Now, a word of caution. If a technical surveillance countermeasures (TSCM) expert pronounces a room secure, it can remain that way only if you protect it from intrusion. This means that you may discuss your trade secrets with reasonable expectation of security right after the TSCM team has left. But before you discuss trade secrets again, you need to do another "tech sweep."

Simple but Cost-Effective Protection

Before we talk about the exotic, let's take a minute to consider a simple, nontechnical measure—personnel security. You can use the resources of personnel security to check every candidate for employment. The results of a background investigation or a pre-employment screen (a records check) might have prevented the hiring of that "Director of Marketing." You can use a cost-benefit analysis or a return-on-investment approach: compare the cost of a background investigation to the cost of providing your marketing strategy to a competitor. Now, back to technical measures.

Arts and Crafts

There are three types of devices used for remote electronic room surveillance: transmitters, microphones, and PLDs, or passive listening devices. A transmitter, or more properly, a transmitting device, contains a microphone, a transmitter, an antenna, and a power source. A high-tech, state-of-the-art clandestine transmitter could be as small as one-quarter inch on each side, with a built-in antenna. Depending on environment, weather, and frequency, it could transmit reliably one-half to three-quarters of a mile.

Microphones, as you probably know, come in just about any configuration you can imagine. Basically, a microphone is either wireless or wired. Next time you watch television notice what I mean. Notice how a person might walk around with a wireless mike in her hand. See if you can spot an external antenna poking out of the bottom. The microphone itself is probably no larger than your thumbnail. The rest of the space is taken up by the circuitry and the battery. Many of the battery-driven devices have an on/off switch to conserve the battery. (By the way, hearing aids can be readily adapted to clandestine use. The microphones and batteries are just the right size.)

Another configuration of a miniature, battery-driven (or "wireless") device might be the "body wires" used by undercover law enforcement agents. The power source on these devices has no switch; you can imagine why.

Wired microphones are a real challenge to emplace. However, they are extremely reliable, provide very high fidelity for recording, and can last indefinitely. Wired microphones are normally powered by a host source. That means that the "buggee" (the person being bugged) provides the electricity so that the "bugger" (the person doing the bugging) can hear everything that the buggee says and does. (We used this type of device for the demonstration on the desk and coffee table in our client's office.)

Passive listening devices do not transmit at all unless they are interrogated or actuated by an outside signal. This makes them impossible to detect except by physical examination. These are good for bugging embassies. And company presidents. And contract negotiators.

The "reasonable expectation of security" mentioned earlier means that, at the time of the technical inspection, no listening devices were active, and that no devices were discovered in the room. But what about the device that may have been substituted for the microphone in your telephone? It is a passive listening device. It can be activated from any telephone in the United States. One would only need to surreptitiously transmit a coded series of tones to the device. The device would then transmit, over the telephone line, all sounds produced in the room. The transmission would be accomplished while the telephone handset is on-hook. (This was the type of device that we put into our client's telephone.)

The really bad news is that today's technology allows an eavesdropper to use your telephone as a transmitter by remote means. Physical connections or modifications are no longer necessary.

Within the same family of PLDs is something called a transponder. It is a dormant transmitter that must be activated by a radio frequency (rf) signal, or a laser beam. Once stimulated in this manner, it transmits all sound from the room in which it is secreted to a remote listening post. Sound familiar? It should. In the news several years ago was something called a cavity resonator transponder. The cavity was in the Great Seal of the United States, in the U.S. Embassy in Moscow. A technical survey team once extracted such a device from a set of ornate bookends. They were on a security director's bookshelf, in Delaware.

Every transmitter must have an antenna. An antenna is cut and trimmed according to the frequency to which it must respond; the length can be "mathematically miniaturized." The micro-mini devices have built-in antennas.

All those electric cords and interior wiring you have in your office are great antennas. Any line that carries alternating current (AC) will carry a radio frequency (rf) signal as well. An example would be the less expensive intercom systems: plug them into the wall outlet and talk. How do you think your conversations are transmitted? Rf on AC!

TRASH IS IN THE EYE OF THE BEHOLDER

I mentioned trash early in this book. Its value to the industrial espionage agent cannot be overemphasized. Here's a story about how valuable trash can be. The president and owner of a small advertising firm, after a series of vicious arguments with his wife, locked her out of their house. Angry and hurt, she went to a friend of hers who worked for a rival firm. They decided to bring the husband to financial ruin.

The woman induced her husband's housemaid to bring her every scrap of paper her husband threw away at home. The woman's friend bribed the cleaning force in the building where the husband's advertising firm was located. Over a few weeks, the charforce provided the friend with fourteen large plastic bags full of trash from the firm. The trash contained not only proposals for clients' ad layouts, but campaign strategies for three clients, and a new positioning strategy for its own services. . . .

As it happened, the husband did not come to financial ruin. But he did lose his company, his home, and a Duesenberg classic automobile. That's as close to ruin as anyone can get.

What does this mean to you? Avoid catastrophe by investing a small amount in capital equipment. Buy a shredder. Shred your documents. Use the stuff for mulch.

INSIDE INFORMATION

The most valuable source of information to the IE agent is the employee, but not necessarily an executive employee. Secretaries, maintenance people, clerks, and purchasing agents all have routine, unrestricted access to information that could be of value to another firm or government. It's easier, safer, and cheaper to subvert an employee than it is to bug a suite of offices. Industrial spies may use the same methods as the SVR (the former KGB): Sex, alcohol, drugs, and money are leading contenders for compromise.

HOW TO PREVENT LOSS

How do you deal with these vulnerabilities? Well, a security awareness program is the first step. You need to let people know the value of selected information, provide written policy for them to protect it, and administer sanctions for violations. One way to get people to understand the danger of "leaky lips" is to show them how their jobs are jeopardized when the competition lives off your secrets.

Don't ever underestimate yourself or your firm as a target for eavesdropping. Think like a spy. If your firm has information that could turn a profit, you may be sharing the information right now with someone who will not share the profit with you.

Appendix B offers resources that will be able to guide you in a security education program.

FORECASTING AND WARNING

I've given you a quick look at industrial espionage today. I've offered suggestions on how to reduce your vulnerability to IE. I now close with observations on where I think industrial espionage is going as we move into the year 2000.

Recent history has shown us that spies can collect any information they want. We have all read that Ames and Pollard and Walker and others devastated the United States with their traitorous activities in political espionage. Industrial espionage doesn't get such publicity, but it does portend disaster.

The interception of telephone communications and the subversion of people will grow as threats to American business. The mouth and the modem are dangerous weapons and need to be controlled. The modem will continue into the twenty-first century to be the greatest boon to espionage. Facsimile machines and computers that are connected to the phone system are a more lucrative source of information than people conversing by telephone.

Automated information is passed by local area networks or wide area networks, and sent via modem to everybody in the world, unwittingly or wittingly. The Internet and Intranets are at once the boon and the bane of our information age. By the year 2000, some members of industry will have adopted NSA-like secrecy for telecommunications. (You'll remember that NSA stands for National Security Agency, fondly called No Such Agency by its admirers. This is the agency charged with intercepting and monitoring worldwide communications. Its success has been founded on breaking the communications codes of nearly every country in the world. That's why it's so good at protecting our own communications: it designs codes that others cannot break.)

American business, by about 2003, may come to realize that the Internet is not a secure means of communication, no matter what its publicists assert. In my opinion, it will never be safe to transmit critical information via Internet or Intranet connections.

By 2003, some firms will have survived as host providers of lucrative information, but only at the pleasure of parasite competitors—much the same as caterpillars survive, paralyzed and zombie-like, becoming food for the young of a wasp. Still others will have succumbed to the surreptitious compromise of their critical and sensitive corporate information, not on the Internet, but via barrooms, trash, and human vulnerabilities.

Digital cash will have taken the place of personal computer checking and credit cards. If I were a hostile collector of your company's information, I would hire a full-time staff to monitor every financial transaction emanating from every telephone in your company. Since every electronic transaction from a personal computer can be intercepted, I could identify the idiosyncrasies and indiscretions of your employees for potential use as pressure points. I could use this information to pressure people into providing company secrets. I could learn about the lifestyles of your executives and their secretaries from their cash transactions, and probably pick up some social intelligence to use for blackmail. I could audit cash transactions that seemed inappropriate, and identify ongoing illicit relationships, either for blackmail, or to recruit and exploit the employee as an inside spy. Cash transactions would be inappropriate if they were in a recurring series of deposits or transfers in amounts disproportionate to the income of the senders.

By 2003, American business will have realized that the way to protect critical business information is by erecting security in depth. Business and industry will have mandated personnel reliability programs for all employees as a means of survival. Business and industry will be using the barriers inherent in preemployment screening, drug testing, and psychological testing in conjunction with physical and information security barriers.

By 2003 American business will clearly understand the implications of the dictum

Information is knowledge. Knowledge is power, control.
People over centuries have killed for power and control.

To survive until then, assume that your company is a target for industrial espionage. Use counterespionage, operations security, and security education to keep what's yours, yours.

Appendix B
Resources

HOW TO SELECT A SECURITY CONSULTANT

By now, you can see how dangerous it is to cut corners in security. Expect security professionals to sell you what you need for adequate protection. Unfortunately, sometimes what you want and what you need are not the same. You must trust your provider to offer you the best protection. And trust comes from knowing that you've chosen the right consultant. Here are five steps to show you how to save time and money by selecting the right consultant.

1. Know your expectations and clearly communicate them. Listen to feedback to insure mutual understanding.
2. Discuss the fee schedule. Determine up front if the fees are within your budget.
3. Make sure that the consultants understand the legal aspects of security; expect them to ask you to bring in your attorney to discuss liability issues.
4. Ask knowledgeable questions. *You can get plenty of material from this book.* Listen to the consultant talk about his or her practice. You may not know much about security, but you have common sense. This person represents the image of the consulting firm. Is their image compatible with that of your company?
5. Examine the expertise of the consultants. What kind of experience and education do they have? Look for credentials, such as the

CPP, that will help you believe in the firm. If there are CPPs, CFEs, or CISSPs in the firm, you have an advantage. (These acronyms are explained below.) You can easily verify their credentials.

What Is a CPP?

The CPP, or Certified Protection Professional, is a formal accreditation granted under the auspices of the American Society for Industrial Security. The CPP may practice in any of the basic areas of loss prevention and security:

- ◆ Emergency planning
- ◆ Investigations
- ◆ Legal aspects
- ◆ Personnel security
- ◆ Physical security
- ◆ Protection of sensitive information
- ◆ Security management
- ◆ Substance abuse
- ◆ Loss prevention
- ◆ Liaison

The CFE is a Certified Fraud Examiner; the CISSP is a Certified Information Systems Security Professional.

How to Distinguish a Salesperson from a Consultant

First find out what the person is really selling. If the individual receives compensation from the sale of products or guard services, the person is not a consultant but rather a salesperson. A salesperson cannot make unbiased recommendations. If someone offers you a free consult, you're talking to a salesperson. The free consult has one purpose: to sell hardware or guard services.

On the other hand, a consultant's stock in trade is time, and only time. You compensate a consultant for the education, training, and experience that he or she brings to bear on your problem. Consultants don't give freebies. The person you're talking to is a consultant if:

1. She's being paid for her time.
2. She started the conversation by asking about your goals.
3. She explains the 5-Step risk assessment, and shows you how it applies to your goals.
4. Her training, education, and experience include such disciplines as law enforcement, security management, investigations, or counterintelligence.
5. She's objective, because her compensation does not depend on your purchase of alarm systems or guard services.

Ask Questions about the Consulting Firm

There are five credentials that you can examine: Professional Memberships, Qualifications, Resources and Relationships, Size of Company, and Fees and Services.

Professional Memberships

These are *individual* memberships. The American Society for Industrial Security (ASIS), the largest of its kind in the world, is a professional and educational association of security practitioners.

The Association of Independent Information Professionals (AIIP) consists of small business owners who provide fee-based information services. People who belong to these organizations can be your knowledge assets.

Qualifications

These are each individual's experience and education credentials. If the person claims a college degree, verify that information. Ask for length of experience, as well as relevance of training. For example, if you need a fraud investigation, the firm should refer you to a Certified Fraud Examiner (CFE), rather than to a CPP.

The quality investigator is one who has mastered the academics of quality research. The private investigator test mandated by most state legislatures does not examine academic credentials or analytic skills. Its purpose is to produce revenue for the state.

If your attorney needs legal support with a matter of negligent hiring, wrongful retention, or premises liability, ask her to talk with a

Certified Protection Professional (CPP). Obtain copies of anything the CPP has published. Ask about his experience in public speaking as well. Then call ASIS and ask for a copy of the requirements for CPP certification.

The CPP, as a specialist in loss prevention management, can be a knowledge asset for you. He can show you how to do a 5-Step Risk Assessment, or show you how spies steal your company secrets.

Resources and Relationships
These are the credentials of the firm as a business or corporate body. Beware of any firm that asserts that it can handle all types of investigations, all types of research, and get on it right away. In today's world, such capabilities bespeak enormous labor cost and fixed expense. If you find a company that claims it will take your case over the phone and get to it immediately, you may have found a company that has no other clients.

Size of Company
If you want all your loss prevention resources under one roof, call a large company. If you want personalized service, retain a small firm. Large, old firms tend to rely on their name for a continuous flow of business. Small firms rely on each client, one at a time.

The size of the company has no relationship to its Knowledge Capital. Knowledge Capital is your return on the information provider's investment in information sources and its expertise within the firm as well as its reach outside the firm. A firm rich in Knowledge Capital offers you added value based on its pool of knowledge. And if you're looking for value-added services, be prepared to pay for them, without regard to the size of the company.

Fees and Services
Consider buying added value, reliability, and credentials, rather than cheap prices. Read each firm's brochures, take notes during phone conversations, and ask questions. Then ask yourself if the firm has credibility.

Beware of the small firm that offers prices that sound too good to be true. Companies that charge cut-rate prices do cut-rate work. Some firms sell information at or below cost. How credible is a company that sells below cost, without charging for its service? Who pays for the labor and overhead? And if the firm is not in business for profit, what is its hidden agenda?

The consequences of dealing with such a company are insidious. You may not realize what has been done to you until you wind up in court. That is why most of us laugh when we hear, "I can get the same thing for half the price." Not in today's world.

THEN ASK YOURSELF, WHY RETAIN A CONSULTANT?

- ♦ You may need an independent, unbiased, frank opinion.
- ♦ You may need specialized expertise, perhaps in debugging, or security education, personnel security, or AIS (automated information systems) security.
- ♦ Or you may need outside support to show management new perspectives in a particularly sensitive situation.

Fraud!

You may need a consultant (such as a Certified Fraud Examiner, or CFE) to assume an investigative or fraud auditor's role. If so, your auditor will conduct a type of program analysis to discover, for example: the weakest links in the chain of control; patterns of deviation from acceptable accounting practice; a simple way to compromise your system; a pattern of write-offs of receivables; opportunities for faked claims, debits, invoices; etc. A CFE may ask you or your controller to answer several pages of critical questions before beginning any investigation or examination of records.

ADDITIONAL RESOURCES

Here's a list of free, or mostly free, sources of information, including brochures, pamphlets, videos, and IBM PC diskettes. Mail your request on your letterhead with a check to Pitorri and Associates, Inc., 5505 Tobego Ct., Fairfax, VA 22032.

When ordering, include your purchase receipt for this book, or a photocopy of page 13 of this book as proof of purchase.

Videos ($5.39 each for postage and handling, except where otherwise noted)

♦ Economic and Industrial Espionage: Piracy in the Twentieth Century (RT 16min 45sec)
♦ Espionage 2000 (RT 30min)
♦ Friend and/or Foe: The New Espionage Challenge (RT 12min 20sec)
♦ Intelligence Threats: The Why of OPSEC (RT 14min 51sec) (Free)
♦ Operations Security—A Different Point of View (RT 30min) Comes with a Facilitator's Guide (Free)
♦ Confidentially Speaking (A film about signal intelligence narrated by Greg Morris) (RT 13 min)
♦ Networks at Risk (RT approx. 11 min)

Diskettes (IBM PC 3 1/2″ only)—Sets of two diskettes for each program (Free)

♦ OPSEC Fundamentals—Computer Based Training. (Goes into details about background and applications of operations security). May be installed on DOS or Windows; set of two diskettes and a manual. Diskettes may be copied.
♦ Introduction to OPSEC—Computer-Based Training. (Animated; very basic, but interesting program.) May be installed on Windows only; set of two diskettes. Diskettes may be copied. (Free)

Brochures and Pamphlets (Free)

♦ Operations Security Program Manager's Handbook
♦ Intelligence Threat Handbook
♦ OPSEC Program Evaluation

Reference Diskettes (3 1/2″ IBM PC only) in ASCII Standard Text

Note: Ask for INFODISK. Postage and handling is $2.65.

♦ Industrial Espionage Act of 1996
♦ Economic Security Act of 1996

♦ Adjudicative Guidelines for Determining Eligibility for Access to Classified Information
♦ Investigative Standards for Background Investigations for Access to Classified Information
♦ Annual Report to Congress: Foreign Economic Collection and Industrial Espionage 1996
♦ Public Attitudes toward Security and Counterespionage Matters in 1994 and 1996
♦ Information Security in a Third Wave Society
♦ Threats to Computer Systems: An Overview
♦ Personal Computer Security Guidelines
♦ Computer Crime Categories: How Techno-Criminals Operate
♦ Management Guide for the Protection of Information Resources

And here's a list of organizations that could be of assistance to you.

American Society for Industrial Security
1655 North Fort Myer Drive, Suite 1200
Arlington, Virginia 22209
703 522-5800

Interagency OPSEC Support Staff
6411 Ivy Lane, Suite 400
Greenbelt, Maryland 20770
301 982-0323

National Security Institute
57 East Main Street, Suite 217
Westborough, Massachusetts 01581
508 366-5800

Department of Defense Security Institute
8000 Jefferson Davis Highway
Richmond, Virginia 23297
804 279-4223

Defense Investigative Service
1340 Braddock Place
Alexandria, Virginia 22314

National Counterintelligence Center
Room 3W01 — NHB
Washington, DC 20505
703 874-4122 or 703 482-8648

Pitorri and Associates, Inc.
Forensic Security Consulting (Liability Issues), Security
Education, Counterespionage, and Fraud Investigations
5505 Tobego Court
Fairfax, Virginia 22032
703 323-7303
FAX: 703 323-7398

Glossary

ACCEPTABLE RISK or ACCEPTABLE LEVEL OF RISK: the potential dollar loss or exposure to legal consequences that you are willing to assume without instituting security measures or purchasing insurance. A deductible is one example of Acceptable Risk: you underwrite that amount yourself, because you are willing to accept that level of exposure to loss.

ACCESS CONTROL: any system (normally electronic) that detects, announces, records, monitors, and prevents or controls passage into or out of a protected area.

ADJUDICATION: a process to provide reasonable assurance that the person being considered meets certain standards, and that the person's future behavior will be in the best interest of the employer. (See also Security)

AIS SECURITY: See Automated Information Systems Security

ASSETS: in security and OPSEC: people; information and physical items of such value as to merit budgeted protection. In counterintelligence: human sources of information.

ASSESSMENT, RISK: an OPSEC process of evaluating the probability of loss based on threat and vulnerability.

AUTOMATED INFORMATION SYSTEMS SECURITY: application of the principles of loss-prevention management to the protection of automated information; the application includes physical, information, and personnel security methods.

AVAILABILITY [of automated information]: state of being accessible for retrieval from a system; usable; the A in CIA (confidentiality, integrity, availability).

BACKGROUND INVESTIGATION (BI):   consists of the collection and adjudication of information about an individual. The collection is performed by interviewing references, educators, relatives, and neighbors; the BI includes an LFC (local files check) and an NAC (national agency check).

BACKGROUND SCREENING: consists of searches of court, employment, education, and other records, usually by computer online sources, but may include letter, telecopy, or telephone for verification; a local files check. See also *Vet*.

BUG: may refer to any type of miniature listening device.

COLLECTION, INTELLIGENCE: the gathering of information from all available sources in order to satisfy specified requirements.

COLLECTION PLATFORMS: sources or methods of intelligence gathering, such as human sources, signal sources, imagery or photographic sources.

COMPROMISE: usually, of information, but also applies to human intelligence sources. Exposed to harm or suspicion of true purpose, as in an agent working undercover may have the cover compromised, exposing him as an espionage agent.

CONFIDENTIALITY [of automated information]:   state of having been generated and maintained in secrecy; the C in CIA (confidentiality, integrity, availability).

DECEPTION: information or activities designed to mislead intelligence collectors.

DEFENSIVE SOURCE OPERATIONS: a specialized counterintelligence activity in which local sources are recruited to observe and report activities; the sources are given no information; they are periodically debriefed.

DELAY TIME: the time necessary for an intruder to penetrate his target; in personnel security, delay time results from employee screening, and provides an employer the time to evaluate an individual without placing the company at risk.

DUE CARE: care that an ordinarily prudent person would have exercised under similar conditions.

ESPIONAGE: the clandestine collection of information about a country other than one's own while in the service of one's own country [one of several usable definitions].

EXPOSURE: the announcement of a person's presence to other persons of lawful authority who can apprehend him, or cause his apprehension, or prevent his entrance into, or remaining within a defined area. Also, the degree to which a person may be held answerable in a court of law or in a court of equity.

HANDLER: a master spy; an experienced agent who manages or "runs" other agents and their sources; now called a case officer.

INFOTERRORISM: symbolic criminal acts of compromise, intrusion, or destruction of automated information, designed to influence an audience beyond the immediate victims.

LIABLE (Liability):   legally bound; answerable; responsible (exposure to court ordered consequences).

LOCAL FILES CHECK: a review of local public records pertaining to an individual; the information is provided by the person, such as a certificate of police in-files check.

LOSS PREVENTION (LP) MANAGEMENT: a body of knowledge whose application to a given environment reduces, eliminates, or controls loss from natural disasters, accident, or malice; LP Management is a multidisciplinary system of control, applying architecture, engineering, fire science, law, management science, and other fields.

NATIONAL AGENCY CHECK (NAC):   a review of information about a person contained in designated agencies in the continental United States; this always includes, but is not limited to, credit, military records, and social security.

NEGLIGENCE: the failure to use such care as a reasonably prudent and careful person would use under similar circumstances.

OFFENSIVE COUNTERINTELLIGENCE OPERATIONS (OFCO): aggressive actions by counterintelligence operators to neutralize espionage activities.

REDUNDANCY [of collection platforms]:   to use more than one means of collecting information or intelligence, usually in order to validate the sources and the information.

RISK: exposure to harm or loss; the state of being in such exposure.

RULE OF PARSIMONY: the expenditure of the least amount of money necessary to attain the proper level of loss prevention (e.g., parsimonious acquisition of security resources: buy only what you need to do the job); the lowest level of defense that will afford adequate protection.

SECURITY: a system of interrelated barriers designed to deter, delay, detect, and report access into, movement within, and egress from a defined area; protection of assets.

SECURITY, INFORMATION: the protection of information assets through application of the principles of information security; reduction of exposure to risk of loss of critical or sensitive information.

SECURITY MANAGEMENT: the application of the principles of loss prevention management to the cost-effective acquisition of security resources; the exercise of control and direction over security resources.

SECURITY, PERSONNEL: barriers in personnel security are those physical activities and reasoning processes used in determining the integrity, suitability, trustworthiness, and honesty of employees and employment candidates (synonymous with background screening).

SECURITY, PHYSICAL: protection barriers, including lights, fences, dogs, locks, intrusion detection systems, and human response to provide extended delay time and exposure; access control.

SOURCE: a source of information, usually a person; a HUMINT, or human intelligence collection platform.

TRADECRAFT: specialized clandestine operations, used to gather intelligence, or to detect and neutralize the gathering of intelligence; usually involves physical and electronic assets.

VET or VETTING [British]:   to subject a person to an appraisal, via a background investigation (BI).

Index